PRAYING THROUGH

THE GOSPEL OF LUKE

A Devotional book of prayers

by Berenice Aguilera

COPYRIGHT

© *2015 Berenice Aguilera*

All rights reserved. No part of this publication may be reproduced, stored in a retrieval system, or transmitted by any means – electronic, mechanical, photographic (photocopying), recording, or otherwise – without prior permission in writing from the author.

ISBN-13: 978-1516851263
ISBN-10: 1516851269

Scripture quoted by permission.
All scripture quotations, unless otherwise indicated, are taken from the NET Bible®
copyright ©1996-2006 by Biblical Studies Press, L.L.C. All rights reserved.

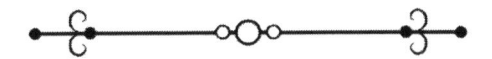

CONTENTS

Introduction 1

Luke's Personal Note to Theophilus 3

Birth of John the Baptist Foretold 4

Birth of Jesus Foretold 7

Mary Visits Elizabeth 9

Mary's Song 11

Birth of John the Baptist 13

Zechariah's Song 15

Birth of Jesus 17

Shepherds and Angels 19

Jesus Presented at the Temple 21

Jesus at the Temple 24

John the Baptist Prepares the Way 26

Baptism and Genealogy of Jesus 29

Jesus is Tempted 31

Jesus Rejected at Nazareth..33

Jesus Drives Out an Evil Spirit..36

Jesus Heals Many...38

Calling of First Disciples..40

The Man With Leprosy...42

Jesus Heals a Paralytic 44

The Calling of Levi..46

Jesus Questioned About Fasting 48

The Twelve Apostles 51

Blessings and Woes 53

Love Your Enemies..55

Judging Others 57

The Tree and Its Fruit...59

Wise and Foolish Builders... 60

The Faith of the Centurion 62

Jesus Raises a Widow's Son 64

Jesus and John the Baptist...66

Jesus Anointed by a Sinful Woman................................69

Parable of the Sower 72

A Lamp on a Stand 75

Jesus' Mother and Brothers 76

Jesus Calms the Storm 78

The Healing of a Demon-possessed Man 80

A Dead Girl and a Sick Woman 83

Jesus Sends Out the Twelve 86

Jesus Feeds the Five Thousand 88

Peter's Confession of Christ 90

The Transfiguration 92

The Healing of a Boy With an Evil Spirit 94

Who Will Be the Greatest? 96

Samaritan Opposition 98

The Cost of Following Jesus 100

Jesus Sends Out the Seventy-two 102

The Parable of the Good Samaritan 105

At the Home of Martha and Mary 108

Jesus' Teaching on Prayer 109

Jesus and Beelzebub 112

The Sign of Jonah 114

The Lamp of the Body 116

Six Woes 117

Warnings and Encouragements 120

The Parable of the Rich Fool 122

Do Not Worry 124

Watchfulness 126

Not Peace but Division 128

Interpreting the Times 130

Repent or Perish 132

A Crippled Woman Healed on the Sabbath 134

The Parables of the Mustard Seed and the Yeast 136

The Narrow Door... 138

Jesus' Sorrow for Jerusalem...140

Jesus at a Pharisee's House 142

The Parable of the Great Banquet 145

The Cost of Being a Disciple 147

The Parable of the Lost Sheep 149

The Parable of the Lost Coin 151

The Parable of the Lost Son 153

The Older Brother 155

The Parable of the Shrewd Manager 157

Additional Teachings 160

The Rich Man and Lazarus 161

Sin Faith, Duty 163

Ten Healed of Leprosy 165

The Coming of the Kingdom of God..167

The Parable of the Persistent Widow 169

The Parable of the Pharisee and the Tax Collector 171

The Rich Ruler 173

Jesus Again Predicts His Death 175

A Blind Beggar Receives His Sight..176

Zacchaeus the Tax Collector... 178

The Parable of the Ten Minas 180

The Triumphal Entry 183

Jesus at the Temple... 185

The Authority of Jesus Questioned... 186

The Parable of the Tenants 188

Paying Taxes to Caesar 190

The Resurrection and Marriage 192

Whose Son Is the Christ? 194

The Widow's Offering 196

Signs of the End of the Age 197

Judas Agrees to Betray Jesus 201

Passover Preparations 203

The Last Supper 205

Who is the Greatest? 207

Jesus Predicts Peter's Denial 209

Jesus Prays on the Mount of Olives 211

Peter Disowns Jesus 213

Jesus Before the Assembly of Elders 215

Jesus Before Pilate and Herod 217

The Crucifixion 220

Jesus' Death and Burial 223

The Resurrection 225

On the Road to Emmaus 227

Jesus Appears to the Disciples 230

The Ascension 232

Also by Berenice Aguilera 233

INTRODUCTION

> *Since, then, you have been raised with Christ, set your hearts on things above, where Christ is, seated at the right hand of God. Set your minds on things above, not on earthly things. For you died, and your life is now hidden with Christ in God. When Christ, who is your life, appears, then you also will appear with him in glory. (Col 3:1-4)*

Where is your heart set? Is it set on heaven.... or is it set on earthly things?

When you took that step and placed your trust and life into God's care; when you took God at His word and chose to believe that Jesus paid the price for your sin; your life became hidden with Christ in God. You belong to Him. And it will take a lifetime and more to get to know Him

> *And now, just as you accepted Christ Jesus as your Lord, you must continue to follow him. Let your roots grow down into him, and let your lives be built on him. Then your faith will grow strong in the truth you were taught, and you will overflow with thankfulness. (Col 2:6-7)*

Question: How do you grow roots into Him? How do you build your life on Him? How do you see your faith grow?

Answer: Such profound questions have an easy answer. Immerse yourself in the Bible.

When Jesus died, the veil of the temple was torn in two making it possible for you to have a personal relationship with Him. It's easy. Just talk to Him. He is your risen Saviour. That's what He came to earth for. You.

As you read through the gospel of Luke, you will find your knowledge of God expanding and growing. You will find that He talks to you through His word. You will find that horrible spiritual dryness disappearing, along with depression and despair. It will change the way you deal with your family, your work situation and relationships in every area of your life. It will be easier to discern His will and clearly see the works He has for you to do.

As you read the Bible and pray, you will experience more moments of joy and peace. You will find strength in circumstances you never thought you could cope with. You will find your life fulfilled and content.

Try and set a time aside each day to pray and read the Bible. Take your time. If there is one thing I have learned over the years, it is that God is never in a hurry! As you pray, if other words come to mind, go with it. This book is meant to be a spring-board to you praying your own prayers and not a collection of set prayers. So off you go, get on your knees.... and pray!

May God bless you and guide you by His Spirit as you seek His presence.

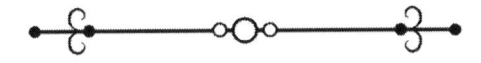

LUKE'S PERSONAL NOTE TO THEOPHILUS
LUKE 1:1-4

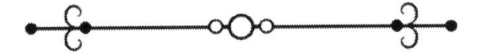

Since many have undertaken to set in order a narrative concerning those matters which have been fulfilled among us, even as those who from the beginning were eyewitnesses and servants of the word delivered them to us, it seemed good to me also, having traced the course of all things accurately from the first, to write to you in order, most excellent Theophilus; that you might know the certainty concerning the things in which you were instructed.

Father, I thank you for your written word. I ask you that as I read through the Gospel of Luke you will open up my heart and my understanding. As I pray through each section please give me grace and wisdom. Draw me close to you. I pray that as you work in my life, and as I too am an eyewitness to your works, that you give me opportunity to share with others. Whether it be by the written word whether it be by spoken word, I ask you that your Gospel might go out and that you will be honoured and glorified.

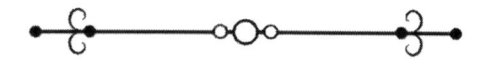

BIRTH OF JOHN THE BAPTIST FORETOLD

LUKE 1:5-23

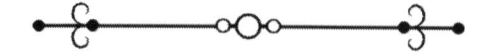

There was in the days of Herod, the king of Judea, a certain priest named Zacharias, of the priestly division of Abijah. He had a wife of the daughters of Aaron, and her name was Elizabeth.

They were both righteous before God, walking blamelessly in all the commandments and ordinances of the Lord. But they had no child, because Elizabeth was barren, and they both were well advanced in years.

Now while he executed the priest's office before God in the order of his division, according to the custom of the priest's office, his lot was to enter into the temple of the Lord and burn incense. The whole multitude of the people were praying outside at the hour of incense.

An angel of the Lord appeared to him, standing on the right side of the altar of incense. Zacharias was troubled when he saw him, and fear fell upon him. But the angel said to him, "Don't be afraid, Zacharias, because your request has been heard, and your wife, Elizabeth, will bear you a son, and you shall call his name John. You will have joy and gladness; and many will rejoice at his birth. For he will be great in the sight of the Lord, and he will drink no wine nor strong drink. He will be filled with the Holy Spirit, even from his mother's womb. He will turn many of the children of Israel to the Lord, their God. He will go before him in the spirit and power of Elijah, 'to turn the hearts of the fathers to the children, and the disobedient to the wisdom of the just; to prepare a people prepared for the Lord."

Zacharias said to the angel, "How can I be sure of this? For I am an old man, and my wife is well advanced in years."

The angel answered him, "I am Gabriel, who stands in the presence of God. I was sent to speak to you, and to bring you this good news. Behold you will be silent and not able to speak, until the day that these things will happen, because you didn't believe my words, which will be fulfilled in their proper time."

The people were waiting for Zacharias, and they marvelled that he delayed in the temple. When he came out, he could not speak to them, and they perceived that he had seen a vision in the temple. He continued making signs to them, and remained mute.

I pray Father that even as Zechariah spent so many years being faithful to you, so I too might spend a life of being faithful to you. I pray that I will grasp with both hands anything you might tell me to do. Root out all unbelief in my life. I want to learn to trust you more. I want my faith to grow. I pray Lord that you will teach me to be obedient to you. Amen

BIRTH OF JESUS FORETOLD

LUKE 1:26-38

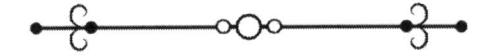

Now in the sixth month, the angel Gabriel was sent from God to a city of Galilee, named Nazareth, to a virgin pledged to be married to a man whose name was Joseph, of David's house. The virgin's name was Mary. Having come in, the angel said to her, "Rejoice, you highly favoured one! The Lord is with you. Blessed are you among women!"

But when she saw him, she was greatly troubled at the saying, and considered what kind of salutation this might be. The angel said to her, "Don't be afraid, Mary, for you have found favour with God. Behold, you will conceive in your womb, and give birth to a son, and will call his name 'Jesus.' He will be great, and will be called the Son of the Most High. The Lord God will give him the throne of his father, David, and he will reign over the house of Jacob forever. There will be no end to his Kingdom."

Mary said to the angel, "How can this be, seeing I am a virgin?"

The angel answered her, "The Holy Spirit will come on you, and the power of the Most High will overshadow you. Therefore also the holy one who is born from you will be called the Son of God. Behold, Elizabeth, your relative, also has conceived a son in her old age; and this is the sixth month with her who was called barren. For nothing spoken by God is impossible."

Mary said, "Behold, the servant of the Lord; let it be done to me according to your word."

The angel departed from her.

○○○◯○○○

Lord, how amazing it must have been for Mary to see the angel, and how faith-filled a response to the message given to her. I pray that your will be done in my life. May it be to me as you will Lord God. May I accept your plans and purposes for my life. Whether it be through hardships and trials, or through easy times, I want my life to be characterised by a faithful heart like Mary. Amen.

MARY VISITS ELIZABETH

LUKE 1:39-45

Mary arose in those days and went into the hill country with haste, into a city of Judah, and entered into the house of Zacharias and greeted Elizabeth.

When Elizabeth heard Mary's greeting, the baby leaped in her womb, and Elizabeth was filled with the Holy Spirit.

She called out with a loud voice, and said, "Blessed are you among women, and blessed is the fruit of your womb! Why am I so favoured, that the mother of my Lord should come to me? For behold, when the voice of your greeting came into my ears, the baby leaped in my womb for joy! Blessed is she who believed, for there will be a fulfillment of the things which have been spoken to her from the Lord!"

Father I want to bring my children before you. I know that before they were born you had a plan and a purpose for their lives. I know that your purpose for the lives of my children will be to your glory.

I ask you that they will love you with all their hearts. I ask you that your word will be rich in their lives. I pray that you will fill them with your Holy Spirit and that they will serve you all the days of their lives. Amen.

MARY'S SONG

LUKE 1:46-56

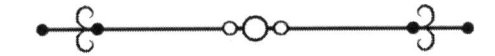

Mary said,
"My soul magnifies the Lord.
My spirit has rejoiced in God my Saviour,
for he has looked at the humble state of his servant.
For behold, from now on, all generations will call me blessed.
For he who is mighty has done great things for me.
Holy is his name.
His mercy is for generations of generations on those who fear him.
He has shown strength with his arm.
He has scattered the proud in the imagination of their hearts.
He has put down princes from their thrones.
And has exalted the lowly.
He has filled the hungry with good things.
He has sent the rich away empty.
He has given help to Israel, his servant, that he might remember mercy,

As he spoke to our fathers,
to Abraham and his offspring forever."

Mary stayed with her about three months, and then returned to her house.

Let your name be glorified my God and Saviour. You looked upon me and chose to reveal yourself to me. Your mercy is truly incredible. Words cannot express how grateful I am that you changed my heart and my life. You extended your hand to me that I might belong to you forever. I know that my future is with you. You are the God who directs the hearts of Kings. You are the God who brings down the proud. You are the God who holds the world in the palm of his hands. I know each breath that I breathe is given by you. I know you direct my paths. Oh God, let my life be a living sacrifice to you, in Jesus name, amen.

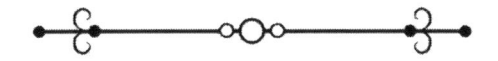

BIRTH OF JOHN THE BAPTIST

LUKE 1:57-66

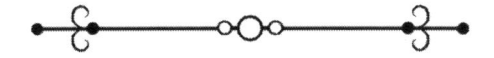

Now the time that Elizabeth should give birth was fulfilled, and she gave birth to a son. Her neighbours and her relatives heard that the Lord had magnified his mercy towards her, and they rejoiced with her. On the eighth day, they came to circumcise the child; and they would have called him Zacharias, after the name of his father. His mother answered, "Not so; but he will be called John."

They said to her, "There is no one among your relatives who is called by this name." They made signs to his father, what he would have him called.

He asked for a writing tablet, and wrote, "His name is John."

They all marvelled. His mouth was opened immediately, and his tongue freed, and he spoke, blessing God. Fear came on all who lived around them, and all these sayings were talked about throughout all the hill country of Judea.

All who heard them laid them up in their heart, saying, "What then will this child be?" The hand of the Lord was with him.

Lord, as I read about the birth of John the Baptist, I see Zechariah and Elizabeth being obedient to you even when it meant going against the traditions of their culture. I see the result of their obedience was their neighbours being filled with awe. Because of his obedience, everyone knew that you were at work. I ask you Lord, no matter what you may ask me to do, no matter how others around me might feel about it, that I will be obedient to what you ask of me. I pray that my obedience to you will bring honour to your name, amen.

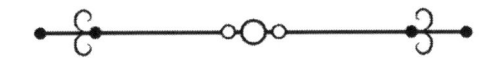

ZECHARIAH'S SONG

LUKE 1:67-80

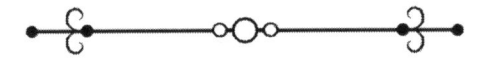

His father, Zacharias, was filled with the Holy Spirit, and prophesied, saying,

"Blessed be the Lord, the God of Israel, for he has visited and redeemed his people; and has raised up a horn of salvation for us in the house of his servant David (as he spoke by the mouth of his holy prophets who have been from of old), salvation from our enemies, and from the hand of all who hate us; to show mercy towards our fathers, to remember his holy covenant, the oath which he swore to Abraham, our father, to grant to us that we, being delivered out of the hand of our enemies, should serve him without fear, In holiness and righteousness before him all the days of our life.

And you, child, will be called a prophet of the Most High, for you will go before the face of the Lord to prepare his ways, to give knowledge of salvation to his people by the remission of their sins, because of the tender mercy of our God, whereby the dawn from on high will visit us, to shine on those who sit in darkness and the shadow of death; to guide our feet into the way of peace."

The child was growing, and becoming strong in spirit, and was in the desert until the day of his public appearance to Israel.

Thank you for the obedience of your prophets of old. What beautiful words describe my wonderful Saviour; holy, righteous, giver of knowledge of salvation, tender and merciful, a light shining in the darkness to guide our feet. Beautiful Saviour, wonderful God, fill me with your Spirit that I might be a beacon to your glory. Amen.

BIRTH OF JESUS

LUKE 2:1-7

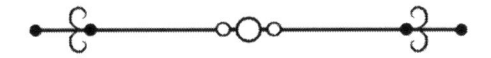

Now in those days, a decree went out from Caesar Augustus that all the world should be enrolled. This was the first enrolment made when Quirinius was governor of Syria. All went to enrol themselves, everyone to his own city. Joseph also went up from Galilee, out of the city of Nazareth, into Judea, to David's city, which is called Bethlehem, because he was of the house and family of David; to enrol himself with Mary, who was pledged to be married to him as wife, being pregnant.

While they were there, the day had come for her to give birth. She gave birth to her firstborn son. She wrapped him in bands of cloth, and laid him in a feeding trough, because there was no room for them in the inn.

Lord Jesus, thank you that you were willing to leave your glory behind. It is incomprehensible to me how you could look upon mankind and decide to save us. Your grace is unfathomable. Who is there like you? From your birth to your death you have been a model of humility and goodness. I ask you Lord, to reveal any areas in my life where pride is still an issue. No matter how painful it may be to me, I want pride rooted out. As I read your word, I ask that you will change me. I pray for humility, and a heart that considers others before myself. Even as you, Lord Jesus, pointed people to the Father, I pray that my life will be one that points people to you. Amen

SHEPHERDS AND ANGELS

LUKE 2:8-20

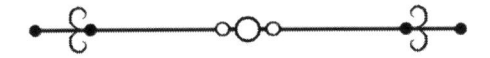

There were shepherds in the same country staying in the field, and keeping watch by night over their flock. Behold, an angel of the Lord stood by them, and the glory of the Lord shone around them, and they were terrified. The angel said to them, "Don't be afraid, for behold, I bring you good news of great joy which will be to all the people. For there is born to you today, in David's city, a Saviour, who is Christ the Lord. This is the sign to you: you will find a baby wrapped in strips of cloth, lying in a feeding trough." Suddenly, there was with the angel a multitude of the heavenly army praising God, and saying,

"Glory to God in the highest, on earth peace, good will toward men."

When the angels went away from them into the sky, the shepherds said to one another, "Let's go to Bethlehem, now, and see this thing that has happened, which the Lord has made known to us." They came with haste, and found both Mary and

Joseph, and the baby was lying in the feeding trough. When they saw it, they publicized widely the saying which was spoken to them about this child. All who heard it wondered at the things which were spoken to them by the shepherds. But Mary kept all these sayings, pondering them in her heart. The shepherds returned, glorifying and praising God for all the things that they had heard and seen, just as it was told them.

ooo◯ooo

O God, I ask your forgiveness for the times when you have spoken to me, and I've ignored what you've said. I know there have been so many opportunities where I failed to speak about you. I've been embarrassed and tongue-tied not knowing what to say. I don't want this in my life. Forgive me Lord God. I pray you will change my heart so I might testify freely. I ask that you would take away all fear of man and what they might think about me. Give me opportunities to speak to others about you. Speak into my life that I might testify to your goodness. Open my dull hearing so I might hear you clearly. Open my understanding so that I might recognise when you're at work. Teach me to ponder your words in my heart. Teach me to praise and glorify your name. Amen.

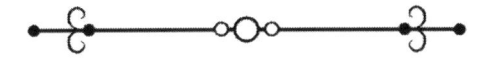

JESUS PRESENTED AT THE TEMPLE

LUKE 2:21-40

When eight days were fulfilled for the circumcision of the child, his name was called Jesus, which was given by the angel before he was conceived in the womb.

When the days of their purification according to the law of Moses were fulfilled, they brought him up to Jerusalem, to present him to the Lord (as it is written in the law of the Lord, "Every male who opens the womb shall be called holy to the Lord"), and to offer a sacrifice according to that which is said in the law of the Lord, "A pair of turtledoves, or two young pigeons."

Behold, there was a man in Jerusalem whose name was Simeon. This man was righteous and devout, looking for the consolation of Israel, and the Holy Spirit was on him. It had been revealed to him by the Holy Spirit that he should not see death before he had seen the Lord's Christ. He came in the Spirit into the temple. When the parents brought in the child, Jesus, that they might do concerning him according to the custom of the law, then he received him into his arms, and blessed God, and said,

"Now you are releasing your servant, Master,
according to your word, in peace;
for my eyes have seen your salvation,
which you have prepared before the face of all peoples;
a light for revelation to the nations,
and the glory of your people Israel."

Joseph and his mother were marveling at the things which were spoken concerning him, and Simeon blessed them, and said to Mary, his mother, "Behold, this child is set for the falling and the rising of many in Israel, and for a sign which is spoken against. Yes, a sword will pierce through your own soul, that the thoughts of many hearts may be revealed."

There was one Anna, a prophetess, the daughter of Phanuel, of the tribe of Asher (she was of a great age, having lived with a husband seven years from her virginity, and she had been a widow for about eighty-four years), who didn't depart from the temple, worshiping with fastings and petitions night and day. Coming up at that very hour, she gave thanks to the Lord, and spoke of him to all those who were looking for redemption in Jerusalem. When they had accomplished all things that were according to the law of the Lord, they returned into Galilee, to their *own city, Nazareth. The child was growing, and was becoming strong in spirit, being filled with wisdom, and the grace of God was upon him.*

○○○○○○○

Father, as I read about Simeon, a righteous and devout man who spent so long faithfully waiting for his Messiah; and Anna, who lived in the temple worshipping night and day and spending her life in prayer and fasting; I long to see these characteristics in my life. I want to be completely immersed in you. I want to love you more and seek you more and know you more. You are my life, my foundation, my strong tower. Without you I know that I am nothing. Without you I cannot draw breath. Instill in me a habit of obedience. Help me to remember to pray more. Help me to remember to bring my problems and needs before you. So often I get wrapped up in them that I forget I have a Father who supplies all my needs and carries my burdens. O God, there is no one like you. Teach me to wait on you in faithfulness and trust like Simeon and Anna. Amen.

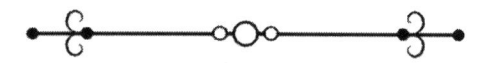

JESUS AT THE TEMPLE

LUKE 2:41-52

His parents went every year to Jerusalem at the feast of the Passover.

When he was twelve years old, they went up to Jerusalem according to the custom of the feast, and when they had fulfilled the days, as they were returning, the boy Jesus stayed behind in Jerusalem. Joseph and his mother didn't know it, but supposing him to be in the company, they went a day's journey, and they looked for him among their relatives and acquaintances. When they didn't find him, they returned to Jerusalem, looking for him. After three days they found him in the temple, sitting in the middle of the teachers, both listening to them, and asking them questions. All who heard him were amazed at his understanding and his answers. When they saw him, they were astonished, and his mother said to him, "Son, why have you treated us this way? Behold, your father and I were anxiously looking for you."

He said to them, "Why were you looking for me? Didn't you know that I must be in my Father's house?" They didn't understand the saying which he spoke to them. And he went down with them, and came to Nazareth. He was subject to them, and his mother kept all these sayings in her heart. And Jesus increased in wisdom and stature, and in favour with God and men.

∞○∞

Lord, Jesus' reply to his mother resonates in my heart. "Didn't you know I must to be about my Father's business?" I too want to be about my Father's business. I want to be able to explain to others the marvels of your word and the hope you have given us. I pray that as I read your word that you will change my heart. Make me more like you. I want to love others and have concern for their welfare, because you do. I want to share the gospel with my neighbours and friends, because you have given me this news and saved me. I pray that even as Mary pondered your words in her heart, that I too would consider your word deeply during the day. Amen.

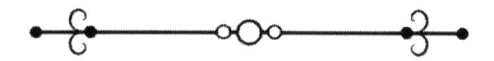

JOHN THE BAPTIST PREPARES THE WAY

LUKE 3:1-20

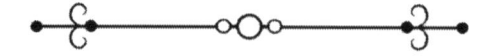

Now in the fifteenth year of the reign of Tiberius Caesar, Pontius Pilate being governor of Judea, and Herod being tetrarch of Galilee, and his brother Philip tetrarch of the region of Ituraea and Trachonitis, and Lysanias tetrarch of Abilene, in the high priesthood of Annas and Caiaphas, the word of God came to John, the son of Zacharias, in the wilderness. He came into all the region around the Jordan, preaching the baptism of repentance for remission of sins. As it is written in the book of the words of Isaiah the prophet,

"The voice of one crying in the wilderness,
'Make ready the way of the Lord.
Make his paths straight.
Every valley will be filled.
Every mountain and hill will be brought low.
The crooked will become straight,
and the rough ways smooth.
All flesh will see God's salvation.'"

He said therefore to the multitudes who went out to be baptized by him, "You offspring of vipers, who warned you to flee from the wrath to come? Therefore produce fruits worthy of repentance, and don't begin to say among yourselves, 'We have Abraham for our father;' for I tell you that God is able to raise up children to Abraham from these stones! Even now the axe also lies at the root of the trees. Every tree therefore that doesn't produce good fruit is cut down, and thrown into the fire."

The multitudes asked him, "What then must we do?"

He answered them, "He who has two coats, let him give to him who has none. He who has food, let him do likewise."

Tax collectors also came to be baptized, and they said to him, "Teacher, what must we do?"

He said to them, "Collect no more than that which is appointed to you."

Soldiers also asked him, saying, "What about us? What must we do?"

He said to them, "Extort from no one by violence, neither accuse anyone wrongfully. Be content with your wages."

As the people were in expectation, and all men reasoned in their hearts concerning John, whether perhaps he was the Christ, John answered them all, "I indeed baptize you with water, but he comes who is mightier than I, the strap of whose sandals I am not worthy to loosen. He will baptize you in the Holy Spirit and fire, whose fan is in his hand, and he will thoroughly cleanse his threshing floor, and will gather the wheat into his barn; but he will burn up the chaff with unquenchable fire."

Then with many other exhortations he preached good news to the people, but Herod the tetrarch, being reproved by him for Herodias, his brother's wife, and for all the evil things which Herod had done, added this also to them all, that he shut up John in prison.

I see in this passage a man who is completely sold out to the work his God has given him. I see no holding back, no fear and no concern for the opinions of others. This is how I want to be, Lord. I want this love for you that casts out all fear. Draw me close to you. Give me words to say to tell those around me about you. I pray that I will be faithful in doing those good works you set before me. Help me to seize every opportunity to do good. Take away all weariness of heart and apathy that so often affects my life. Fill me with your Holy Spirit and guide me into your truth. In Jesus name, Amen.

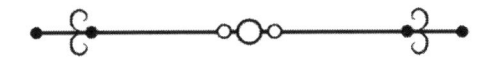

BAPTISM AND GENEALOGY OF JESUS

LUKE 3:21-38

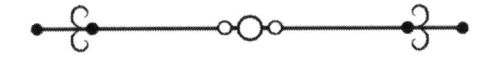

Now when all the people were baptized, Jesus also had been baptized, and was praying. The sky was opened, and the Holy Spirit descended in a bodily form like a dove on him; and a voice came out of the sky, saying "You are my beloved Son. In you I am well pleased."

Jesus himself, when he began to teach, was about thirty years old, being the son (as was supposed) of Joseph, the son of Heli, the son of Matthat, the son of Levi, the son of Melchi, the son of Jannai, the son of Joseph, the son of Mattathias, the son of Amos, the son of Nahum, the son of Esli, the son of Naggai, the son of Maath, the son of Mattathias, the son of Semein, the son of Joseph, the son of Judah, the son of Joanan, the son of Rhesa, the son of Zerubbabel, the son of Shealtiel, the son of Neri, the son of Melchi, the son of Addi, the son of Cosam, the son of Elmodam, the son of Er, the son of Jose, the son of Eliezer, the son of Jorim, the son of Matthat, the son of Levi, the son of Simeon, the son of Judah, the son of Joseph, the son of Jonan, the son of Eliakim, the son of Melea, the son of Menan, the son of Mattatha, the son of Nathan, the son of David, the son of Jesse, the son of Obed, the son of Boaz, the son of Salmon, the son of Nahshon, the son of Amminadab, the son of Aram,‡ the son of Hezron, the son of Perez, the son of Judah, the son of Jacob, the son of Isaac, the son of Abraham, the son of Terah, the son of Nahor, the son of Serug, the son of Reu, the son of Peleg, the son of Eber, the son of Shelah, the son of Cainan, the son of Arphaxad, the son of Shem, the son of Noah, the son of Lamech, the son of Methuselah, the son of Enoch, the son of Jared, the son of Mahalaleel, the son of Cainan, the son of Enos, the son of Seth, the son of Adam, the son of God.

∞∞○∞∞

Thank you Lord Jesus that you came down to earth to save us from our sin. Thank you that you have made me a part of your family; so I might have the privilege of calling your Father, my Father too. You humbled yourself even to getting baptised, when in truth, you had no need. I pray that you will soften my heart and make me sensitive to your voice. I ask that my life might be an example to those around me, thus pointing them to you. Thank you that the Spirit that came upon you when you were baptized, is the same Spirit that lives within me, leading and guiding me. I love you so much and want you to be lifted up in my life. You are my God and I worship you. Amen.

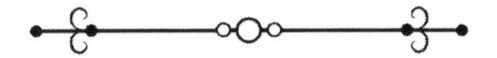

JESUS IS TEMPTED

LUKE 4:1-13

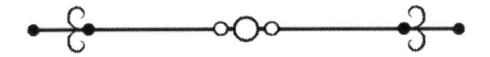

Jesus, full of the Holy Spirit, returned from the Jordan, and was led by the Spirit into the wilderness for forty days, being tempted by the devil. He ate nothing in those days. Afterward, when they were completed, he was hungry. The devil said to him, "If you are the Son of God, command this stone to become bread."

Jesus answered him, saying, "It is written, 'Man shall not live by bread alone, but by every word of God.'"

The devil, leading him up on a high mountain, showed him all the kingdoms of the world in a moment of time. The devil said to him, "I will give you all this authority, and their glory, for it has been delivered to me; and I give it to whomever I want. If you therefore will worship before me, it will all be yours."

Jesus answered him, "Get behind me Satan! For it is written, 'You shall worship the Lord your God, and you shall serve him only.'"

He led him to Jerusalem, and set him on the pinnacle of the temple, and said to him, "If you are the Son of God, cast yourself down from here, for it is written,

'He will put his angels in charge of you, to guard you;'

and,

*'On their hands they will bear you up,
lest perhaps you dash your foot against a stone.' "*

Jesus answering, said to him, "It has been said, 'You shall not tempt the Lord your God.' "

When the devil had completed every temptation, he departed from him until another time.

∞∞○∞∞

I know Father in this life you allow trials and difficulties in order to strengthen our faith and develop perseverance. I pray that you will increase my desire for your word, so it might indeed be my daily bread. I pray that you will make me aware when other things creep in my life and threaten to take that place that should only be yours. You are my God and you are the only One I want to serve. I don't want to find myself being sidetracked by making something into an idol. I also ask for wisdom so that I might never put you to the test. Make me aware when I am proud and being a 'know-all.' Give me strength to overcome the temptations of the devil. I just want a humble heart to serve you in spirit and in truth. I ask these things in Jesus name. Amen.

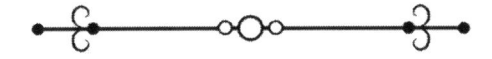

JESUS REJECTED AT NAZARETH

LUKE 4:14-30

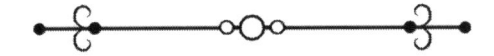

Jesus returned in the power of the Spirit into Galilee, and news about him spread through all the surrounding area. He taught in their synagogues, being glorified by all.

He came to Nazareth, where he had been brought up. He entered, as was his custom, into the synagogue on the Sabbath day, and stood up to read. The book of the prophet Isaiah was handed to him. He opened the book, and found the place where it was written,

"The Spirit of the Lord is on me,
because he has anointed me to preach good news to
the poor.
He has sent me to heal the broken hearted,
to proclaim release to the captives,
recovering of sight to the blind,
to deliver those who are crushed,
and to proclaim the acceptable year of the Lord."

He closed the book, gave it back to the attendant, and sat down. The eyes of all in the synagogue were fastened on him. He began to tell them, "Today, this Scripture has been fulfilled in your hearing."

All testified about him, and wondered at the gracious words which proceeded out of his mouth, and they said, "Isn't this Joseph's son?"

He said to them, "Doubtless you will tell me this parable, 'Physician, heal yourself! Whatever we have heard done at Capernaum, do also here in your hometown.'" He said, "Most certainly I tell you, no prophet is acceptable in his hometown. But truly I tell you, there were many widows in Israel in the days of Elijah, when the sky was shut up three years and six months, when a great famine came over all the land. Elijah was sent to none of them, except to Zarephath, in the land of Sidon, to a woman who was a widow. There were many lepers in Israel in the time of Elisha the prophet, yet not one of them was cleansed, except Naaman, the Syrian."

They were all filled with wrath in the synagogue, as they heard these things. They rose up, threw him out of the city, and led him to the brow of the hill that their city was built on, that they might throw him off the cliff. But he, passing through the middle of them, went his way.

Father I ask that the richness of your word permeate every area of my life. Words cannot express how grateful I am that you had mercy on me and revealed yourself to me. You have set me free from the law of sin and death and opened my blind eyes to your amazing grace. O God let there be no unbelief found in my life. Root out any area where I lack trust and deal with it. I want no hindrance to your purposes in my life. Send me where you will. Use me as you will. Gift me with words that I might tell others of your wonderful love. You are truly a loving Father and I love you. Amen.

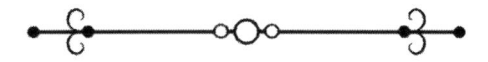

Jesus Drives Out an Evil Spirit

Luke 4:31-37

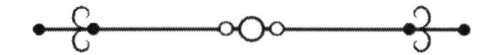

He came down to Capernaum, a city of Galilee. He was teaching them on the Sabbath day, and they were astonished at his teaching, for his word was with authority. In the synagogue there was a man who had a spirit of an unclean demon, and he cried out with a loud voice, saying, "Ah! what have we to do with you, Jesus of Nazareth? Have you come to destroy us? I know you who you are: the Holy One of God!"

Jesus rebuked him, saying, "Be silent, and come out of him!" When the demon had thrown him down in the middle of them, he came out of him, having done him no harm.

Amazement came on all, and they spoke together, one with another, saying, "What is this word? For with authority and power he commands the unclean spirits, and they come out!" News about him went out into every place of the surrounding region.

Lord Jesus, I pray that when faced with the work of the devil you will give me discernment and courage whether to cast out a demon or not. I am so ignorant in these matters and feel really out of my depth when thinking about them. As I read your word, draw me close to you that I might not miss your prompting in wanting to set someone free. I know that I often miss listening to you properly and only later realise that it was you talking to me. Help me to recognise your voice. Let me not be so busy and unaware that I miss what you are trying to tell me. I want my life to be lived wholly for you. Please help me Lord, Amen.

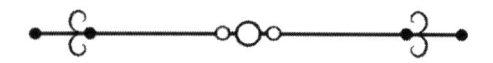

JESUS HEALS MANY

LUKE 4:38-44

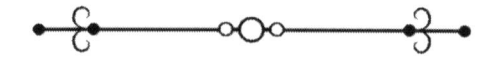

He rose up from the synagogue, and entered into Simon's house. Simon's mother-in-law was afflicted with a great fever and they begged him for her. He stood over her, and rebuked the fever; and it left her. Immediately she rose up and served them. When the sun was setting, all those who had any sick with various diseases brought them to him; and he laid his hands on every one of them, and healed them. Demons also came out of many, crying out, and saying, "You are the Christ, the Son of God!" Rebuking them, he didn't allow them to speak, because they knew that he was the Christ.

When it was day, he departed and went into an uninhabited place, and the multitudes looked for him, and came to him, and held on to him, so that he wouldn't go away from them. But he said to them, "I must preach the good news of God's Kingdom to the other cities also. For this reason I have been sent." He was preaching in the synagogues of Galilee.

Lord Jesus, I would love to pray for people and see them healed. Would you grant me that joy of seeing people healed by the power of your name? I pray again for any unbelief in my life to be rooted out. I know it is nothing to do with me when people are healed. It is by your divine power and mercy that lives are touched. Lord please use me to bring others to you, whether it be by praying for healing, or sharing your deep love for them. I want to bring honour to you. I want to see unbelievers bowing the knee before you and come into your kingdom. I ask this in your holy name, Amen.

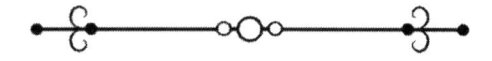

CALLING OF FIRST DISCIPLES

LUKE 5:1-11

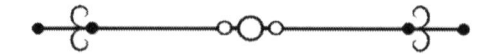

Now while the multitude pressed on him and heard the word of God, he was standing by the lake of Gennesaret. He saw two boats standing by the lake, but the fishermen had gone out of them, and were washing their nets. He entered into one of the boats, which was Simon's, and asked him to put out a little from the land. He sat down and taught the multitudes from the boat. When he had finished speaking, he said to Simon, "Put out into the deep, and let down your nets for a catch."

Simon answered him, "Master, we worked all night, and took nothing; but at your word I will let down the net." When they had done this, they caught a great multitude of fish, and their net was breaking. They beckoned to their partners in the other boat, that they should come and help them. They came, and filled both boats, so that they began to sink. But Simon Peter, when he saw it, fell down at Jesus' knees, saying, "Depart from me, for I am a sinful man, Lord." For he was amazed, and all who were with him, at the catch of fish which they had caught; and so also were James and John, sons of Zebedee, who were partners with Simon.

Jesus said to Simon, "Don't be afraid. From now on you will be catching people alive."

When they had brought their boats to land, they left everything, and followed him.

∞∞○∞∞

O God, I ask you for an obedient and compliant heart. When you ask me to do something, I pray that I might straight away get up and do it, without hesitation or procrastination. I see Simon, James and John leaving everything because you asked them to follow you. What an incredible example. They had only just met you and didn't know anything about you, yet they trusted. Forgive me for the many times I have ignored your voice and gone my own way. Forgive me my ignorance and lack of trust. Change my heart Lord. Give me a heart of obedience and faith. I pray that I might recognise your voice and respond instantly, in Jesus name I pray, Amen.

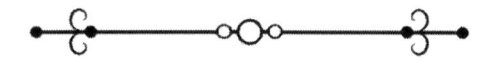

The Man With Leprosy

Luke 5:12-16

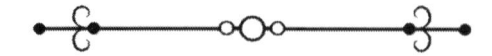

While he was in one of the cities, behold, there was a man full of leprosy. When he saw Jesus, he fell on his face, and begged him, saying, "Lord, if you want to, you can make me clean."

He stretched out his hand, and touched him, saying, "I want to. Be made clean."

Immediately the leprosy left him. He commanded him to tell no one, "But go your way, and show yourself to the priest, and offer for your cleansing according to what Moses commanded, for a testimony to them." But the report concerning him spread much more, and great multitudes came together to hear, and to be healed by him of their infirmities. But he withdrew himself into the desert, and prayed.

Father I pray that you will give me compassion for those in need. Let me not walk by and ignore someone, when you would wish me to stop and bring words of life to that person's life. Use me to bless those around me. I want to spend more time with you seeking your face. As I read how Jesus often withdrew to lonely places to pray, I am convicted at my lack of desire to do the same. I truly want my life to be immersed in you. Please help me to set more time aside to seek your face. Please help and strengthen me in my weakness and apathy. I know I lack so much and all I need to do is ask. I am ashamed my life is so full of things to do, that often I have no time for you. Forgive me. I don't want this in my life. I want the opposite. I want to seek your face and listen for your voice and be obedient in everything you ask. Help me Father to come aside and be alone with you. Amen.

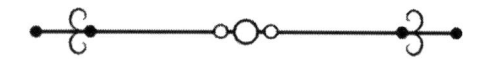

JESUS HEALS A PARALYTIC

LUKE 5:17-26

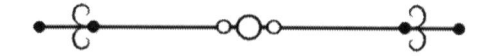

On one of those days, he was teaching; and there were Pharisees and teachers of the law sitting by, who had come out of every village of Galilee, Judea, and Jerusalem. The power of the Lord was with him to heal them. Behold, men brought a paralyzed man on a cot, and they sought to bring him in to lay before Jesus. Not finding a way to bring him in because of the multitude, they went up to the housetop, and let him down through the tiles with his cot into the middle before Jesus. Seeing their faith, he said to him, "Man, your sins are forgiven you."

The scribes and the Pharisees began to reason, saying, "Who is this that speaks blasphemies? Who can forgive sins, but God alone?"

But Jesus, perceiving their thoughts, answered them, "Why are you reasoning so in your hearts? Which is easier to say, 'Your sins are forgiven you;' or to say, 'Arise and walk?' But that you may know that the Son of Man has authority on earth to forgive sins" (he said to the paralyzed man), "I tell you, arise, and take up your cot, and go to your house."

Immediately he rose up before them, and took up that which he was laying on, and departed to his house, glorifying God. Amazement took hold on all, and they glorified God. They were filled with fear, saying, "We have seen strange things today."

∞∞O∞∞

O God, you alone have the power over sickness and sin. You alone can heal and forgive. Thank you for forgiving me and making me righteous in your sight. I ask for faith like the friends of the paralytic man. I see them acting according to that faith, and I see your name being lifted up. I want this in my life. I want to do the works you ask me to do, whether it means praying for the sick, or loving the unlovable, or standing up in faith when there is unbelief around me. I want to do your will. Use me in your service Father. Show me what you would have me do. Give me awareness of the good works you set before me and let not a time go by that I ignore that call. I ask this in Jesus name, Amen.

THE CALLING OF LEVI

LUKE 5:27-32

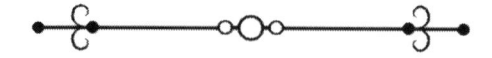

After these things he went out, and saw a tax collector named Levi sitting at the tax office, and said to him, "Follow me!"

He left everything, and rose up and followed him. Levi made a great feast for him in his house. There was a great crowd of tax collectors and others who were reclining with them. Their scribes and the Pharisees murmured against his disciples, saying, "Why do you eat and drink with the tax collectors and sinners?" Jesus answered them, "Those who are healthy have no need for a physician, but those who are sick do. I have not come to call the righteous, but sinners to repentance."

Lord Jesus, let me never go past someone thinking they are too unimportant for you to care about. Give me courage to talk to the beggar and the stranger. Use me to bring your light into lives full of darkness and despair. Give me the joy of seeing a life turned around, from sinner to saved. I long to talk to my friends and family about you; I feel so inadequate when opportunities come along and I find myself tongue-tied, not knowing what to say. Please help me as I read and listen to your word, not just to understand it in my heart, but be able to explain your amazing gift of salvation. Amen

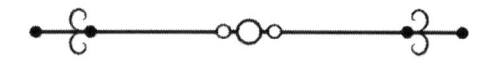

JESUS QUESTIONED ABOUT FASTING

LUKE 5:33 - LUKE 6:11

They said to him, "Why do John's disciples often fast and pray, likewise also the disciples of the Pharisees, but yours eat and drink?"

He said to them, "Can you make the friends of the bridegroom fast, while the bridegroom is with them? But the days will come when the bridegroom will be taken away from them. Then they will fast in those days." He also told a parable to them. "No one puts a piece from a new garment on an old garment, or else he will tear the new, and also the piece from the new will not match the old. No one puts new wine into old wine skins, or else the new wine will burst the skins, and it will be spilled, and the skins will be destroyed. But new wine must be put into fresh wine skins, and both are preserved. No man having drunk old wine immediately desires new, for he says, 'The old is better.'"

Now on the second Sabbath after the first, he was going through the grain fields. His disciples plucked the heads of grain and ate, rubbing them in their hands. But some of the Pharisees said to them, "Why do you do that which is not lawful to do on the Sabbath day?"

Jesus, answering them, said, "Haven't you read what David did when he was hungry, he, and those who were with him; how he entered into God's house, and took and ate the show bread, and gave also to those who were with him, which is not lawful to eat except for the priests alone?" He said to them, "The Son of Man is lord of the Sabbath."

It also happened on another Sabbath that he entered into the synagogue and taught. There was a man there, and his right hand was withered. The scribes and the Pharisees watched him, to see whether he would heal on the Sabbath, that they might find an accusation against him. But he knew their thoughts; and he said to the man who had the withered hand, "Rise up, and stand in the middle." He arose and stood. Then Jesus said to them, "I will ask you something: Is it lawful on the Sabbath to do good, or to do harm? To save a life, or to kill?" He looked around at them all, and said to the man, "Stretch out your hand." He did, and his hand was restored as sound as the other. But they were filled with rage, and talked with one another about what they might do to Jesus.

Father, let me never fall into the trap of thinking that my actions affect my salvation, rather my salvation is secure because of the cross. Please reveal to me if there is any area of empty religion in my life, that I need to turn away from. I know my works mean nothing when it comes to your grace. I know that I am saved because of Jesus death on the cross, and the penalty has been paid for my sin. There is nothing I can add that will make me more saved. I am so grateful to you for having mercy on me. I am so thankful that you took me out of my sin and shame and turned my life around. I want my life to be such that it points people to you. I want my speech to glorify your name, and my heart to be one of constant worship. In Jesus name I pray, Amen.

THE TWELVE APOSTLES

LUKE 6:12-16

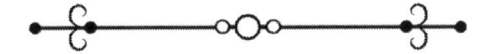

In these days, he went out to the mountain to pray, and he continued all night in prayer to God. When it was day, he called his disciples, and from them he chose twelve, whom he also named apostles: Simon, whom he also named Peter; Andrew, his brother; James; John; Philip; Bartholomew; Matthew; Thomas; James, the son of Alphaeus; Simon, who was called the Zealot; Judas the son of James; and Judas Iscariot, who also became a traitor.

O God, I pray that my heart might be faithful and filled with longing for your presence. I pray that even when I've had a full day, when I am tired and washed out you will give me the strength to turn to you and draw my strength from you. Please help me to pray. Teach me to praise you for your goodness and the joy you bring to my life. Thank-you that even as you chose the disciples, you also chose me. I cannot find the words to express how honoured I feel. Just as they were not random choices made on a whim, but chosen deliberately, I too was chosen by you. My heart is full of gratefulness and thankfulness. Who is like you, O Lord my God? There is NONE like you. Amen.

BLESSINGS AND WOES

LUKE 6:17-26

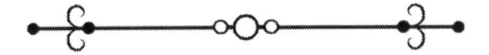

He came down with them, and stood on a level place, with a crowd of his disciples, and a great number of the people from all Judea and Jerusalem, and the sea coast of Tyre and Sidon, who came to hear him and to be healed of their diseases; as well as those who were troubled by unclean spirits, and they were being healed. All the multitude sought to touch him, for power came out of him and healed them all.

He lifted up his eyes to his disciples, and said,
"Blessed are you who are poor,
God's Kingdom is yours.
Blessed are you who hunger now,
for you will be filled.
Blessed are you who weep now,
for you will laugh.

Blessed are you when men shall hate you, and when they shall exclude and mock you, and throw out your name as evil, for the Son of Man's sake.

Rejoice in that day, and leap for joy, for behold, your reward is great in heaven, for their fathers did the same thing to the prophets.

"But woe to you who are rich!
For you have received your consolation.
Woe to you, you who are full now,
for you will be hungry.
Woe to you who laugh now,
for you will mourn and weep.
Woe, when men speak well of you,
for their fathers did the same thing to the false prophets.

∞○∞

Lord God, your compassion and wisdom know no end. Lord Jesus, you touched everyone who came to you. You saw their need and healed them, or cast out demons, or spoke words that changed their lives. I pray that you will work in me that I might be your hands that touch people, your mouth that prays for healing and takes authority over demons to set people free. I pray for wisdom of speech that will turn people's hearts and lives to you. Let my life bring you glory, in Jesus name, Amen.

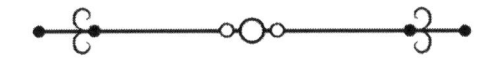

LOVE YOUR ENEMIES

LUKE 6:27-36

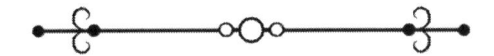

"But I tell you who hear: love your enemies, do good to those who hate you, bless those who curse you, and pray for those who mistreat you. To him who strikes you on the cheek, offer also the other; and from him who takes away your cloak, don't withhold your coat also. Give to everyone who asks you, and don't ask him who takes away your goods to give them back again.

"As you would like people to do to you, do exactly so to them. If you love those who love you, what credit is that to you? For even sinners love those who love them. If you do good to those who do good to you, what credit is that to you? For even sinners do the same. If you lend to those from whom you hope to receive, what credit is that to you? Even sinners lend to sinners, to receive back as much. But love your enemies, and do good, and lend, expecting nothing back; and your reward will be great, and you will be children of the Most High; for he is kind toward the unthankful and evil.

"Therefore be merciful,
even as your Father is also merciful.

∘∘∘○∘∘∘

Help me, Lord, to love those who don't like me, or even hate me. Help me show love and compassion to those I dislike. O God, I forgive *[name the person you need to forgive]* for what he has done against me. I leave him in your hands. Open his heart to you and work your salvation in his life. Change my heart O God. Give me compassion and soften my hard heart. Help me to care instead of being indifferent. Let me desire to actively do good, when I feel like walking past and doing nothing. Help me to change Lord. Amen.

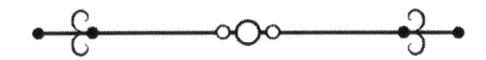

JUDGING OTHERS

LUKE 6:37-42

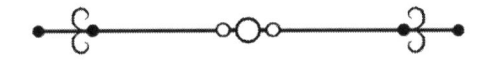

Don't judge, and you won't be judged.
Don't condemn, and you won't be condemned.
Set free, and you will be set free.

"Give, and it will be given to you: good measure, pressed down, shaken together, and running over, will be given to you. For with the same measure you measure it will be measured back to you."

He spoke a parable to them. "Can the blind guide the blind? Won't they both fall into a pit? A disciple is not above his teacher, but everyone when he is fully trained will be like his teacher. Why do you see the speck of chaff that is in your brother's eye, but don't consider the beam that is in your own eye? Or how can you tell your brother, 'Brother, let me remove the speck of chaff that is in your eye,' when you yourself don't see the beam that is in your own eye? You hypocrite! First remove the beam from your own eye, and then you can see clearly to remove the speck of chaff that is in your brother's eye.

Lord, forgive me for the many times I have self-righteously judged others and thought myself better than they were. I desire a humble heart. Help me to realize when I am doing this, and to stop. Help me instead to reach out in your name to them. Forgive me for the many times I have not forgiven others and instead chosen to hold onto hurt, instead of trusting you. I don't want this in my life. Forgive me for the many times I have been selfish and ungenerous. Please change my heart that I might have genuine concern and love for others, instead of walking by uncaring. In Jesus name I pray, Amen.

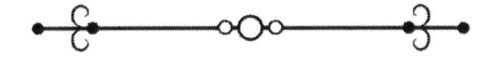

THE TREE AND ITS FRUIT

LUKE 6:43-45

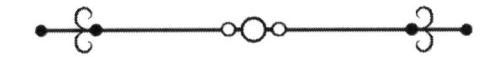

For there is no good tree that produces rotten fruit; nor again a rotten tree that produces good fruit. For each tree is known by its own fruit. For people don't gather figs from thorns, nor do they gather grapes from a bramble bush. The good man out of the good treasure of his heart brings out that which is good, and the evil man out of the evil treasure of his heart brings out that which is evil, for out of the abundance of the heart, his mouth speaks.

Thank-you Lord God that you sent your son Jesus to free me from the punishment I know I deserve. I know I once was rotten. Thank-you for washing me clean and giving me new life. I know there is so much in my life that needs changing. I am yours to do with as you will. Let the fruit of my life be good. Let my speech be grace filled, and not rash, hurtful or plain silly. Let my actions be a blessing. Amen.

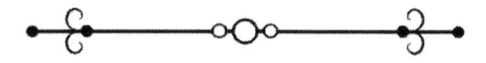

WISE AND FOOLISH BUILDERS

LUKE 6:46-49

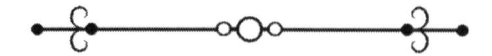

"Why do you call me, 'Lord, Lord,' and don't do the things which I say? Everyone who comes to me, and hears my words, and does them, I will show you who he is like.

He is like a man building a house, who dug and went deep, and laid a foundation on the rock. When a flood arose, the stream broke against that house, and could not shake it, because it was founded on the rock.

But he who hears, and doesn't do, is like a man who built a house on the earth without a foundation, against which the stream broke, and immediately it fell, and the ruin of that house was great."

Lord, I know you are my foundation. I know in times of trouble and distress, when I turn to you, I find hope and comfort. I also know when I forget and wallow in my pain, life seems without hope or meaning. Thank you there is not a second of the day you are not with me. Help me to desire your word. Help me to understand and to act on what I read. Lord, I don't want to be a person pushed one way and then another by an uncertain tide. I want my life to be a testimony to being built on you. I don't want to be swayed when trouble comes, but I want to remain steadfast in hope and sure of your deliverance. Amen.

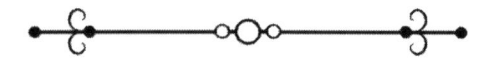

THE FAITH OF THE CENTURION

LUKE 7:1-10

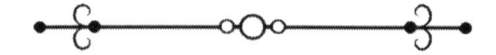

After he had finished speaking in the hearing of the people, he entered into Capernaum. A certain centurion's servant, who was dear to him, was sick and at the point of death. When he heard about Jesus, he sent to him elders of the Jews, asking him to come and save his servant.

When they came to Jesus, they begged him earnestly, saying, "He is worthy for you to do this for him, for he loves our nation, and he built our synagogue for us." Jesus went with them.

When he was now not far from the house, the centurion sent friends to him, saying to him, "Lord, don't trouble yourself, for I am not worthy for you to come under my roof. Therefore I didn't even think myself worthy to come to you; but say the word, and my servant will be healed. For I also am a man placed under authority, having under myself soldiers. I tell this one, 'Go!' and he goes; and to another, 'Come!'

and he comes; and to my servant, 'Do this,' and he does it."

When Jesus heard these things, he marvelled at him, and turned and said to the multitude who followed him, "I tell you, I have not found such great faith, no, not in Israel." Those who were sent, returning to the house, found that the servant who had been sick was well.

<hr />

Lord Jesus, I want to have faith like the Centurion. I want to understand your authority and grace as he must have done. I know that I am so far from this kind of faith. Please give me the grace to believe for more. Open the eyes of my understanding when I read your word, not for knowledge only, but to a deep trust of you. O God, forgive me my unbelief. Forgive me for the many times I have neither turned to you, nor trusted you with my burdens. Please show me where I lack, that I might grow in faith. I want to be able to testify to your goodness and work in my life and I know that lack of faith limits what I can share. Please help me grow in faith. I ask in Jesus name, Amen.

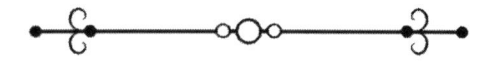

JESUS RAISES A WIDOW'S SON

LUKE 7:11-17

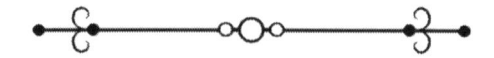

Soon afterwards, he went to a city called Nain. Many of his disciples, along with a great multitude, went with him. Now when he came near to the gate of the city, behold, one who was dead was carried out, the only son of his mother, and she was a widow. Many people of the city were with her.

When the Lord saw her, he had compassion on her, and said to her, "Don't cry." He came near and touched the coffin, and the bearers stood still. He said, "Young man, I tell you, arise!" He who was dead sat up, and began to speak. And he gave him to his mother.

Fear took hold of all, and they glorified God, saying, "A great prophet has arisen among us!" and, "God has visited his people!" This report went out concerning him in the whole of Judea, and in all the surrounding region.

Lord God, I praise your holy name. You love us so much. You see the troubled and those in despair and your heart goes out to them. Thank you that you don't just 'walk on by' ignoring the pain of others, instead you reach out in compassion to heal and provide. You alone are worthy of all honour and glory. Your name is higher than any other. I worship you my Lord and God. Amen.

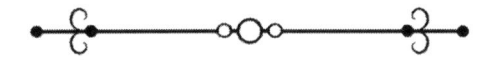

JESUS AND JOHN THE BAPTIST

LUKE 7:18-35

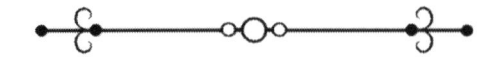

The disciples of John told him about all these things. John, calling to himself two of his disciples, sent them to Jesus, saying, "Are you the one who is coming, or should we look for another?" When the men had come to him, they said, "John the Baptizer has sent us to you, saying, 'Are you he who comes, or should we look for another?'"

In that hour he cured many of diseases and plagues and evil spirits; and to many who were blind he gave sight. Jesus answered them, "Go and tell John the things which you have seen and heard: that the blind receive their sight, the lame walk, the lepers are cleansed, the deaf hear, the dead are raised up, and the poor have good news preached to them. Blessed is he who finds no occasion for stumbling in me."

When John's messengers had departed, he began to tell the multitudes about John, "What did you go out into the wilderness to see? A reed shaken by the wind? But what did you go out to see? A man clothed in soft clothing? Behold, those who are gorgeously dressed, and live delicately, are in kings' courts. But what did you go out to see? A prophet? Yes, I tell you, and much more than a prophet. This is he of whom it is written,

'Behold, I send my messenger before your face,
who will prepare your way before you.'

"For I tell you, among those who are born of women there is not a greater prophet than John the Baptizer, yet he who is least in God's Kingdom is greater than he."

When all the people and the tax collectors heard this, they declared God to be just, having been baptized with John's baptism. But the Pharisees and the lawyers rejected the counsel of God, not being baptized by him themselves.

"To what then should I compare the people of this generation? What are they like? They are like children who sit in the marketplace, and call to one another, saying, 'We piped to you, and you didn't dance. We mourned, and you didn't weep.' For John the Baptizer came neither eating bread nor drinking wine, and you say, 'He has a demon.' The Son of Man has come eating and drinking, and you say, 'Behold, a gluttonous man, and a drunkard; a friend of tax collectors and sinners!' Wisdom is justified by all her children."

Thank you Lord that you are patient with our unbelief and our doubts. You don't turn away from us in frustration and impatience when yet again we question your will or the path our lives are taking. I pray for acceptance of your will in my life. Lord, I WILL trust in you whether the path be smooth and easy, or whether you lead me through times of pain and suffering. I know that your way is right. I know that your way leads to joy and fulfilment. I especially know that your way leads to praise being given to your name. This is what I want in my life. Amen

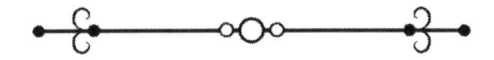

Jesus Anointed by a Sinful Woman

Luke 7:36-50

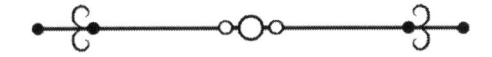

One of the Pharisees invited him to eat with him. He entered into the Pharisee's house, and sat at the table.

Behold, a woman in the city who was a sinner, when she knew that he was reclining in the Pharisee's house, brought an alabaster jar of ointment. Standing behind at his feet weeping, she began to wet his feet with her tears, and she wiped them with the hair of her head, kissed his feet, and anointed them with the ointment.

Now when the Pharisee who had invited him saw it, he said to himself, "This man, if he were a prophet, would have perceived who and what kind of woman this is who touches him, that she is a sinner."

Jesus answered him, "Simon, I have something to tell you."

He said, "Teacher, say on."

"A certain lender had two debtors. The one owed five hundred denarii, and the other fifty. When they couldn't pay, he forgave them both. Which of them therefore will love him most?"

Simon answered, "He, I suppose, to whom he forgave the most."

He said to him, "You have judged correctly." Turning to the woman, he said to Simon, "Do you see this woman? I entered into your house, and you gave me no water for my feet, but she has wet my feet with her tears, and wiped them with the hair of her head. You gave me no kiss, but she, since the time I came in, has not ceased to kiss my feet. You didn't anoint my head with oil, but she has anointed my feet with ointment. Therefore I tell you, her sins, which are many, are forgiven, for she loved much. But to whom little is forgiven, the same loves little." He said to her, "Your sins are forgiven."

Those who sat at the table with him began to say to themselves, "Who is this who even forgives sins?"

He said to the woman, "Your faith has saved you. Go in peace."

<hr>

As I read about this wonderful woman showing her love for you even though it meant being humiliated before men, I am reminded of the times in my life where I have behaved like a Pharisee; full of self-righteousness and pride, instead of having a meek and contrite heart. Forgive me Father for my pride and arrogance. Give me a humble heart that I might serve you. I want you to be lifted up in my life, no matter what others say or think about me. Your opinion is what is important. I want to love you in every circumstance without shame or embarrassment. Please change me so that I might serve and honour you like this woman did. Amen.

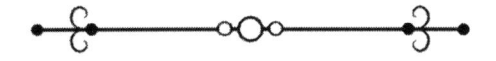

Parable of the Sower

Luke 8:1-15

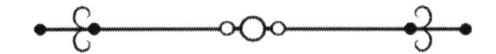

Soon afterwards, he went about through cities and villages, preaching and bringing the good news of God's Kingdom. With him were the twelve, and certain women who had been healed of evil spirits and infirmities: Mary who was called Magdalene, from whom seven demons had gone out; and Joanna, the wife of Chuzas, Herod's steward; Susanna; and many others; who served them from their possessions. When a great multitude came together, and people from every city were coming to him, he spoke by a parable. "The farmer went out to sow his seed. As he sowed, some fell along the road, and it was trampled underfoot, and the birds of the sky devoured it. Other seed fell on the rock, and as soon as it grew, it withered away, because it had no moisture. Other fell amid the thorns, and the thorns grew with it, and choked it. Other fell into the good ground, and grew, and produced one hundred times as much fruit." As he said these things, he called out, "He who has ears to hear, let him hear!"

Then his disciples asked him, "What does this parable mean?"

He said, "To you it is given to know the mysteries of God's Kingdom, but to the rest in parables; that 'seeing they may not see, and hearing they may not understand.' Now the parable is this: The seed is the word of God. Those along the road are those who hear, then the devil comes, and takes away the word from their heart, that they may not believe and be saved. Those on the rock are they who, when they hear, receive the word with joy; but these have no root, who believe for a while, then fall away in time of temptation. That which fell among the thorns, these are those who have heard, and as they go on their way they are choked with cares, riches, and pleasures of life, and bring no fruit to maturity. Those in the good ground, these are those who with an honest and good heart, having heard the word, hold it tightly, and produce fruit with perseverance.

oooO-ooo

Father, I pray for my town. I pray you will bring your words into the lives of people living here. I pray for my family, my friends and neighbours – let your gospel set them free from sin and death. I pray for the Christians here, please fill us with your Spirit, that we might have courage to boldly declare the good news of your incredible love and salvation. I pray for hearts that are prepared to receive your word, so that as we speak, there will be a wonderful response. Give us, O God, the joy of seeing people give their lives into your hands. Give us the joy, O God, of seeing our churches full with newly saved saints hungry for a deep abiding knowledge of your word. I pray for people who are willing to be deeply rooted in your truth, not just seeking an emotional high. In Jesus name I pray, Amen.

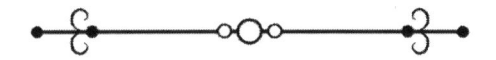

A Lamp on a Stand

Luke 8:16-17

"No one, when he has lit a lamp, covers it with a container, or puts it under a bed; but puts it on a stand, that those who enter in may see the light. For nothing is hidden, that will not be revealed; nor anything secret, that will not be known and come to light.

Lord, I want my heart to be good and noble, as it says in your word. I want to *hear* you. I want to recognise your voice. I pray you will help me to persevere in faith. I pray that I might wrestle with what I don't understand rather than let it go by without bothering. I ask that I will grow in knowing you. Let my heart be filled with joy at your word – and especially I pray that your word in my life will draw others to you. I ask this in Jesus wonderful name, Amen.

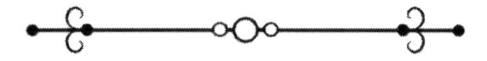

JESUS' MOTHER AND BROTHERS

LUKE 8:18-21

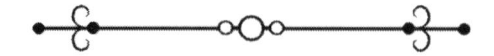

Be careful therefore how you hear. For whoever has, to him will be given; and whoever doesn't have, from him will be taken away even that which he thinks he has."

His mother and brothers came to him, and they could not come near him for the crowd. Some people told him, "Your mother and your brothers stand outside, desiring to see you."

But he answered them, "My mother and my brothers are these who hear the word of God, and do it."

Father, I love you. I worship you. I honour you. You are my firm foundation. Without you I cannot even draw breath. Thank you that I don't have to wait in a crowd to speak to you. Thank you that I don't have to wait my turn before you hear me. I feel so privileged to have access into your presence all the time. Again I ask that you will open my understanding that I might hear you. Again I ask that I might recognise your voice when you speak.

Soften my heart that I might not just hear, but also do as you ask. Lord I am willing to do anything for you. Take my life and do as you will. In Jesus name I pray, Amen.

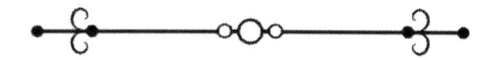

JESUS CALMS THE STORM

LUKE 8:22-25

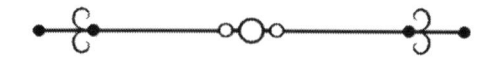

Now on one of those days, he entered into a boat, himself and his disciples, and he said to them, "Let's go over to the other side of the lake." So they launched out. But as they sailed, he fell asleep. A wind storm came down on the lake, and they were taking on dangerous amounts of water. They came to him, and awoke him, saying, "Master, master, we are dying!" He awoke, and rebuked the wind and the raging of the water, and they ceased, and it was calm. He said to them, "Where is your faith?" Being afraid they marvelled, saying to one another, "Who is this then, that he commands even the winds and the water, and they obey him?"

Thank you Lord Jesus that in your presence there is always safety. Thank you that when all around me seems to be difficulties and stress, in the midst you are there calling me to have faith in you. Help me to believe O God, and please forgive the many times I have panicked like the disciples, not truly believing you can help. I know that in times where it seems like being in the valley of the shadow of death, you are with me. Your word is my comfort and my guide. Lord let my testimony to others be of your faithfulness and goodness in my life. Thank you that in difficult times you teach me to trust you. I want to learn to trust you more O God, and if you need to lead me through difficult paths in order to teach me, then I am willing. I know your work in my life is to your glory. Let your will be done. Amen.

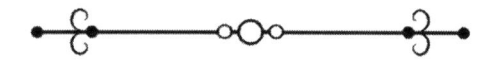

THE HEALING OF A DEMON-POSSESSED MAN

LUKE 8:26-39

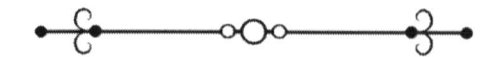

They arrived at the country of the Gadarenes, which is opposite Galilee.

When Jesus stepped ashore, a certain man out of the city who had demons for a long time met him. He wore no clothes, and didn't live in a house, but in the tombs. When he saw Jesus, he cried out, and fell down before him, and with a loud voice said, "What do I have to do with you, Jesus, you Son of the Most High God? I beg you, don't torment me!" For Jesus was commanding the unclean spirit to come out of the man. For the unclean spirit had often seized the man. He was kept under guard, and bound with chains and fetters. Breaking the bonds apart, he was driven by the demon into the desert.

Jesus asked him, "What is your name?"

He said, "Legion," for many demons had entered into him. They begged him that he would not command them to go into the abyss. Now there was there a herd of many pigs feeding on the mountain, and they begged him that he would allow them to enter into those. He allowed them. The demons came out of the man, and entered into the pigs, and the herd rushed down the steep bank into the lake, and were drowned. When those who fed them saw what had happened, they fled, and told it in the city and in the country.

People went out to see what had happened. They came to Jesus, and found the man from whom the demons had gone out, sitting at Jesus' feet, clothed and in his right mind; and they were afraid. Those who saw it told them how he who had been possessed by demons was healed. All the people of the surrounding country of the Gadarenes asked him to depart from them, for they were very much afraid. He entered into the boat, and returned. But the man from whom the demons had gone out begged him that he might go with him, but Jesus sent him away, saying, "Return to your house, and declare what great things God has done for you." He went his way, proclaiming throughout the whole city what great things Jesus had done for him.

∞∞○∞∞

Lord Jesus, in you can be found freedom. In you chains are broken and burdens lifted. In you I can walk without fear of guilt. Thank you for taking the punishment on the cross that I deserve so that I might be free. I cannot understand your mercy or compassion, all I can be is grateful that you extended that mercy to me. I ask you to move in power in my life. I ask that you give me opportunity to tell others what you have done. Please help me to understand you more and to share what I learn with others. I pray for [*unsaved friend/family*]. Please set him free from sin and death to. I pray you give me the joy of leading him to you. I ask in your holy name, Amen.

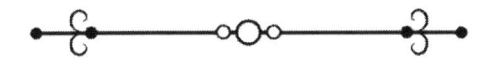

A Dead Girl and a Sick Woman

Luke 8:40-56

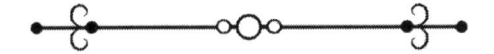

When Jesus returned, the multitude welcomed him, for they were all waiting for him. Behold, there came a man named Jairus, and he was a ruler of the synagogue. He fell down at Jesus' feet, and begged him to come into his house, for he had an only daughter, about twelve years of age, and she was dying. But as he went, the multitudes pressed against him. A woman who had a flow of blood for twelve years, who had spent all her living on physicians, and could not be healed by any, came behind him, and touched the fringe of his cloak, and immediately the flow of her blood stopped. Jesus said, "Who touched me?"

When all denied it, Peter and those with him said, "Master, the multitudes press and jostle you, and you say, 'Who touched me?'"

But Jesus said, "Someone did touch me, for I perceived that power has gone out of me." When the woman saw that she was not hidden, she came trembling, and falling down before him declared to him in the presence of all the people the reason why she had touched him, and how she was healed immediately. He said to her, "Daughter, cheer up. Your faith has made you well. Go in peace."

While he still spoke, one from the ruler of the synagogue's house came, saying to him, "Your daughter is dead. Don't trouble the Teacher."

But Jesus hearing it, answered him, "Don't be afraid. Only believe, and she will be healed."

When he came to the house, he didn't allow anyone to enter in, except Peter, John, James, the father of the child, and her mother. All were weeping and mourning her, but he said, "Don't weep. She isn't dead, but sleeping."

They were ridiculing him, knowing that she was dead. But he put them all outside, and taking her by the hand, he called, saying, "Child, arise!" Her spirit returned, and she rose up immediately. He commanded that something be given to her to eat. Her parents were amazed, but he commanded them to tell no one what had been done.

ooo⚬ooo

Lord God, I am humbled as I read about this woman's suffering, and the way she was so determined to touch you. I am ashamed for the many times I have not made any effort to read your word, or sought you. I am ashamed of my apathy and lack of care. Please forgive me Lord. I don't want this kind of attitude in my life. I want to be determined to seek you. I want to persevere without giving up. Please help me to overcome my apathy. Fill me with your Spirit. Give me zeal for you and your kingdom. Let me love your word more than anything else. I ask this in Jesus name, Amen.

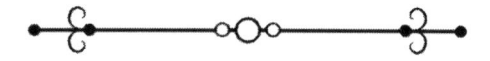

JESUS SENDS OUT THE TWELVE

LUKE 9:1-9

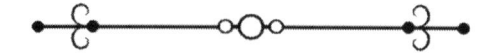

He called the twelve together, and gave them power and authority over all demons, and to cure diseases. He sent them out to preach God's Kingdom and to heal the sick.

He said to them, "Take nothing for your journey— neither staffs, nor wallet, nor bread, nor money; neither have two coats each. Into whatever house you enter, stay there, and depart from there. As many as don't receive you, when you depart from that city, shake off even the dust from your feet for a testimony against them."

They departed, and went throughout the villages, preaching the Good News, and healing everywhere.

Now Herod the tetrarch heard of all that was done by him; and he was very perplexed, because it was said by some that John had risen from the dead, and by some that Elijah had appeared, and by others that one of the old prophets had risen again. Herod said,

"John I beheaded, but who is this, about whom I hear such things?" He sought to see him.

∞∞⟨⟩∞∞

Lord Jesus, I am reminded as I read these scriptures that you have a plan and purpose for the lives of each believer. Our lives are not aimless and purposeless, but instead we have a goal and a calling to follow you as you guide us. Thank you for giving my life purpose. Please help me to be open to wherever and whatever you call me to. Help me to take every opportunity that presents itself to share with others the wonderful news of your great salvation. And help me to reach out in kindness and compassion to those in need and to pray with them. I pray for an obedient heart, in Jesus name, Amen.

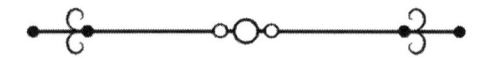

Jesus Feeds the Five Thousand

Luke 9:10-17

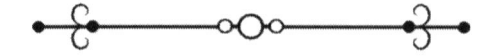

The apostles, when they had returned, told him what things they had done.

He took them, and withdrew apart to a desert region of a city called Bethsaida. But the multitudes, perceiving it, followed him. He welcomed them, and spoke to them of God's Kingdom, and he cured those who needed healing. The day began to wear away; and the twelve came, and said to him, "Send the multitude away, that they may go into the surrounding villages and farms, and lodge, and get food, for we are here in a deserted place."

But he said to them, "You give them something to eat."

They said, "We have no more than five loaves and two fish, unless we should go and buy food for all these people." For they were about five thousand men.

He said to his disciples, "Make them sit down in groups of about fifty each." They did so, and made them all sit down. He took the five loaves and the two fish, and looking up to the sky, he blessed them, and broke them, and gave them to the disciples to set before the multitude. They ate, and were all filled. They gathered up twelve baskets of broken pieces that were left over.

○○○◯○○○

Thank you Lord there is no situation that is too hard for you to deal with. And there is no circumstance where we should forget about your grace and great mercy. Please help me to remember to turn to you first when circumstances become difficult to see if you would reveal yourself instead of me 'fixing' things my way. The disciples wanted to do the 'sensible' thing, but you wanted to reveal yourself to the people. You changed many people's lives that day by feeding them miraculously. Please let me not be blind or deaf should you want to use me to serve those around me. I pray that you will be glorified in my actions and that my life will point constantly to you. I love you so much O God. Amen.

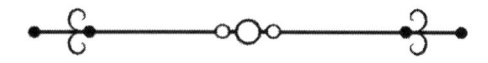

Peter's Confession of Christ

Luke 9:18-27

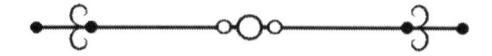

As he was praying alone, the disciples were with him, and he asked them, "Who do the multitudes say that I am?"

They answered, "'John the Baptizer,' but others say, 'Elijah,' and others, that one of the old prophets is risen again."

He said to them, "But who do you say that I am?"

Peter answered, "The Christ of God."

But he warned them, and commanded them to tell this to no one, saying, "The Son of Man must suffer many things, and be rejected by the elders, chief priests, and scribes, and be killed, and the third day be raised up."

He said to all, "If anyone desires to come after me, let him deny himself, take up his cross, and follow me. For whoever desires to save his life will lose it, but whoever will lose his life for my sake, the same will save it. For what does it profit a man if he gains the whole world, and loses or forfeits his own self? For whoever will be ashamed of me and of my words, of him will the Son of Man be ashamed, when he comes in his glory, and the glory of the Father, and of the holy angels. But I tell you the truth: There are some of those who stand here, who will in no way taste of death, until they see God's Kingdom."

∞∞○∞∞

With Peter, I too declare that you are the Christ, you are Lord over all. I am so grateful to you that you opened my heart that I might believe in you. Thank you for your work in my life, and in the life of my family. Thank you that you suffered in my place so that I might be made right before the Father. I cannot put into words how much I want to understand more about what you have done for me. I know there is so much I don't understand, and that what I do understand is so shallow. Teach me more Lord God. Teach me to take up my cross daily and follow you. Change my heart, so that I will not fear embarrassment when sharing about you, but instead trust that you will give me the words to say. Let my life be immersed completely in you, in Jesus name, Amen.

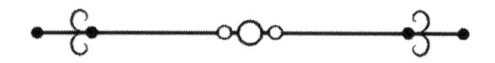

THE TRANSFIGURATION

LUKE 9:28-36

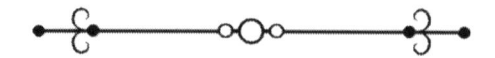

About eight days after these sayings, he took with him Peter, John, and James, and went up onto the mountain to pray. As he was praying, the appearance of his face was altered, and his clothing became white and dazzling. Behold, two men were talking with him, who were Moses and Elijah, who appeared in glory, and spoke of his departure, which he was about to accomplish at Jerusalem.

Now Peter and those who were with him were heavy with sleep, but when they were fully awake, they saw his glory, and the two men who stood with him. As they were parting from him, Peter said to Jesus, "Master, it is good for us to be here. Let's make three tents: one for you, and one for Moses, and one for Elijah," not knowing what he said.

While he said these things, a cloud came and overshadowed them, and they were afraid as they entered into the cloud. A voice came out of the cloud, saying, "This is my beloved Son. Listen to him!" When the voice came, Jesus was found alone. They were silent, and told no one in those days any of the things which they had seen.

∞∞○∞∞

As I read this passage three things jump out at me; You took your disciples aside to pray, they saw your glory, and then the Father telling the disciples to listen to His Son. Help me Lord to set time aside to pray. Help me not to fill my days with so much that I don't have time to talk to you. Give me the desire to seek your presence and help me to be quiet before you and to listen. I know I lack so much in these areas. I want to see your glory Lord; I long for the day when I will see your face and to be with you forever. I want my life to be one of listening to your Son. Teach me to learn. Teach me to study. Teach me to seek you. Amen.

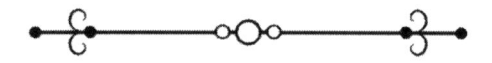

THE HEALING OF A BOY WITH AN EVIL SPIRIT

LUKE 9:37-45

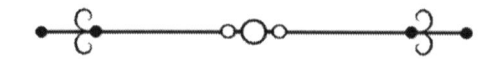

On the next day, when they had come down from the mountain, a great multitude met him. Behold, a man from the crowd called out, saying, "Teacher, I beg you to look at my son, for he is my only child. Behold, a spirit takes him, he suddenly cries out, and it convulses him so that he foams, and it hardly departs from him, bruising him severely. I begged your disciples to cast it out, and they couldn't."

Jesus answered, "Faithless and perverse generation, how long shall I be with you and bear with you? Bring your son here."

While he was still coming, the demon threw him down and convulsed him violently. But Jesus rebuked the unclean spirit, and healed the boy, and gave him back to his father. They were all astonished at the majesty of God.

But while all were marveling at all the things which Jesus did, he said to his disciples, "Let these words sink into your ears, for the Son of Man will be delivered up into the hands of men." But they didn't understand this saying. It was concealed from them, that they should not perceive it, and they were afraid to ask him about this saying.

∞∞○∞∞

Lord Jesus, your compassion is never-ending, your mercy and love are unfathomable. While you were here on earth, so many people wanted you to do things for them and never once did you turn anyone away. You were never too tired, or too busy or too uninterested to stretch out your hand and deliver those suffering from sickness. There is nothing that can stand before your word. Demons HAVE to flee at your command. Sickness HAS to leave at your rebuke. Lord God, there is none like you.

Lord I want to ask you to help me listen for your voice when I read your word. I pray that you will not hide anything from me, but instead help me to understand and grasp what you are saying. I ask this in your holy name, Jesus, Amen.

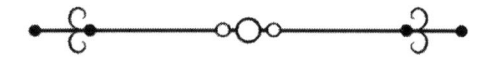

WHO WILL BE THE GREATEST?

LUKE 9:46-50

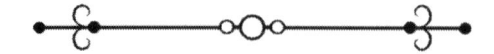

There arose an argument among them about which of them was the greatest. Jesus, perceiving the reasoning of their hearts, took a little child, and set him by his side, and said to them, "Whoever receives this little child in my name receives me. Whoever receives me receives him who sent me. For whoever is least among you all, this one will be great."

John answered, "Master, we saw someone casting out demons in your name, and we forbade him, because he doesn't follow with us."

Jesus said to him, "Don't forbid him, for he who is not against us is for us."

Father, forgive me for the many times I've had the same prideful attitude as the disciples. Forgive me for the many times I have sought to put myself first and not thought of my children, husband or friends. I am ashamed how self-centered I am. Lord, I ask you to change my heart. Help me to see the need in the lives of those around me. Help me to care more. I want to be compassionate and patient. I want to be loving and kind. I pray you will change my heart and mind to be more like your Son. In His name I pray, Amen.

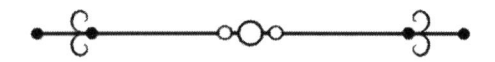

Samaritan Opposition

Luke 9:51-56

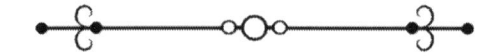

It came to pass, when the days were near that he should be taken up, he intently set his face to go to Jerusalem, and sent messengers before his face. They went, and entered into a village of the Samaritans, so as to prepare for him. They didn't receive him, because he was travelling with his face set towards Jerusalem. When his disciples, James and John, saw this, they said, "Lord, do you want us to command fire to come down from the sky, and destroy them, just as Elijah did?"

But he turned and rebuked them, "You don't know of what kind of spirit you are. For the Son of Man didn't come to destroy men's lives, but to save them."

They went to another village.

Lord Jesus, as I read this passage I see how determined you were to go to the cross. I see how you were unwavering in your decision to save us. Even when the disciples called for you to give the

Samaritans what they truly deserved (indeed what we all deserve), you had mercy on them and showed them grace. You were single-minded in purpose and I am so grateful to you. Because of you my life is changed. Because of the cross and your great mercy, I have hope and I know that my future is secure. There is nothing I need fear. You provide for my every need. And more than that, you have given me yourself. I love you Lord, Amen.

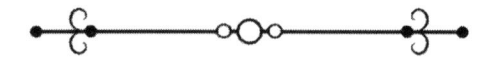

THE COST OF FOLLOWING JESUS

LUKE 9:57-62

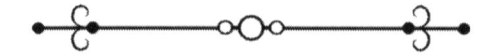

As they went on the way, a certain man said to him, "I want to follow you wherever you go, Lord."

Jesus said to him, "The foxes have holes, and the birds of the sky have nests, but the Son of Man has no place to lay his head."

He said to another, "Follow me!"

But he said, "Lord, allow me first to go and bury my father."

But Jesus said to him, "Leave the dead to bury their own dead, but you go and announce God's Kingdom."

Another also said, "I want to follow you, Lord, but first allow me to say good-bye to those who are at my house."

But Jesus said to him, "No one, having put his hand to the plough, and looking back, is fit for God's Kingdom."

○○○◯○○○

O God, when you asked the disciples to follow you, they immediately left what they were doing and followed. They did not ask any questions, or think about joining you later when they finished with their task. They just obeyed without question. I want this to be my attitude too. I want to read your word and be willing to obey no matter what. Lord God, show me if there are things in my life you wish me to give up. I will give them up and not turn back. Show me if any attitudes are wrong, and I will immediately turn away and obey. Help me to want to do this Father. I want you to be Lord of my whole life, not just in bits and pieces. I see the amazing work you did in the lives of the disciples because they were obedient and trusted you no matter the cost. I want to see your work continue in my life. Help me O God to be obedient, in Jesus name, Amen.

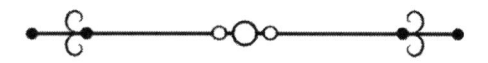

JESUS SENDS OUT THE SEVENTY-TWO

LUKE 10:1-24

Now after these things, the Lord also appointed seventy others, and sent them two by two ahead of him into every city and place, where he was about to come. Then he said to them, "The harvest is indeed plentiful, but the labourers are few. Pray therefore to the Lord of the harvest, that he may send out labourers into his harvest. Go your ways. Behold, I send you out as lambs among wolves. Carry no purse, nor wallet, nor sandals. Greet no one on the way. Into whatever house you enter, first say, 'Peace be to this house.' If a son of peace is there, your peace will rest on him; but if not, it will return to you. Remain in that same house, eating and drinking the things they give, for the labourer is worthy of his wages. Don't go from house to house. Into whatever city you enter, and they receive you, eat the things that are set before you. Heal the sick who are therein, and tell them, 'God's Kingdom has come near to you.' But into whatever city you enter, and they don't receive you, go out into its streets and say, 'Even the dust from your city that clings to us, we wipe off against you. Nevertheless know this, that God's Kingdom has come near to you.'

  I tell you, it will be more tolerable in that day for Sodom than for that city.

"Woe to you, Chorazin! Woe to you, Bethsaida! For if the mighty works had been done in Tyre and Sidon which were done in you, they would have repented long ago, sitting in sackcloth and ashes. But it will be more tolerable for Tyre and Sidon in the judgment than for you. You, Capernaum, who are exalted to heaven, will be brought down to Hades. Whoever listens to you listens to me, and whoever rejects you rejects me. Whoever rejects me rejects him who sent me."

 The seventy returned with joy, saying, "Lord, even the demons are subject to us in your name!"

He said to them, "I saw Satan having fallen like lightning from heaven. Behold, I give you authority to tread on serpents and scorpions, and over all the power of the enemy. Nothing will in any way hurt you. Nevertheless, don't rejoice in this, that the spirits are subject to you, but rejoice that your names are written in heaven."

In that same hour Jesus rejoiced in the Holy Spirit, and said, "I thank you, O Father, Lord of heaven and earth, that you have hidden these things from the wise and understanding, and revealed them to little children. Yes, Father, for so it was well-pleasing in your sight."

Turning to the disciples, he said, "All things have been delivered to me by my Father. No one knows who the Son is, except the Father, and who the Father is, except the Son, and he to whomever the Son desires to reveal him."

Turning to the disciples, he said privately, "Blessed are the eyes which see the things that you see, for I tell you that many prophets and kings desired to see the things which you see, and didn't see them, and to hear the things which you hear, and didn't hear them."

Father, I am so privileged to know you. Thank you that you sent Jesus. Thank you that you chose to reveal yourself to me. I am so very grateful. Lord Jesus you told your disciples that there were few workers, and the same is true today. All around there are people hungry and thirsty for you. Please use me. I am willing to speak of your love and what you have done for us. I ask that you give me opportunities to share my faith with people I come into contact with. I ask that you will prepare hearts to hear your word. O God, give me wisdom and understanding so I might explain clearly what it is you have done for mankind. Lord God, bring more workers to my town. Let your word spread like wildfire. Glorify yourself among us, in Jesus name, Amen.

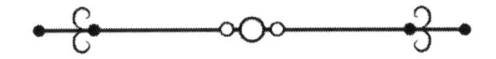

The Parable of the Good Samaritan

Luke 10:25-37

Behold, a certain lawyer stood up and tested him, saying, "Teacher, what shall I do to inherit eternal life?"

He said to him, "What is written in the law? How do you read it?"

He answered, "You shall love the Lord your God with all your heart, with all your soul, with all your strength, and with all your mind; and your neighbour as yourself."

He said to him, "You have answered correctly. Do this, and you will live."

But he, desiring to justify himself, asked Jesus, "Who is my neighbour?"

Jesus answered, "A certain man was going down from Jerusalem to Jericho, and he fell among robbers, who both stripped him and beat him, and departed, leaving him half dead.

By chance a certain priest was going down that way. When he saw him, he passed by on the other side.

In the same way a Levite also, when he came to the place, and saw him, passed by on the other side.

But a certain Samaritan, as he travelled, came where he was. When he saw him, he was moved with compassion, came to him, and bound up his wounds, pouring on oil and wine. He set him on his own animal, and brought him to an inn, and took care of him.

On the next day, when he departed, he took out two denarii, and gave them to the host, and said to him, 'Take care of him. Whatever you spend beyond that, I will repay you when I return.' Now which of these three do you think seemed to be a neighbour to him who fell among the robbers?"

He said, "He who showed mercy on him."

Then Jesus said to him, "Go and do likewise."

Lord God, I know that there have been many times in my life where I have behaved like the priest and the Levite. I have walked on past a person in need because I either could not be bothered, or I was just too busy to notice. I know that you put good deeds before us to do. I don't want to mess up on things you want me to do. Please help me to *see* clearly. Show me again who you want me to help, or listen to, or befriend. I don't want to ignore any direction you give. Forgive me for the times I have not paid attention, or just plain decided not to obey. I don't want this attitude in my life. I want to be obedient in everything you call me to do, in Jesus name, Amen.

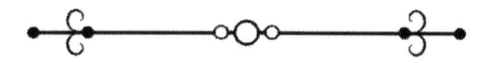

AT THE HOME OF MARTHA AND MARY

LUKE 10:38-42

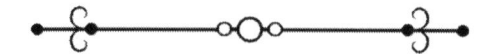

As they went on their way, he entered into a certain village, and a certain woman named Martha received him into her house. She had a sister called Mary, who also sat at Jesus' feet, and heard his word. But Martha was distracted with much serving, and she came up to him, and said, "Lord, don't you care that my sister left me to serve alone? Ask her therefore to help me."

Jesus answered her, "Martha, Martha, you are anxious and troubled about many things, but one thing is needed. Mary has chosen the good part, which will not be taken away from her."

I love you Father. Mould my heart to be open and loving to those in need. Give me a heart like Martha's to open my home and bless those around me. Help me to love as you love me. O God, give me a heart like Mary's that my one purpose is to listen to you. Help me to put aside the business of life and take the time to be in your presence. I ask this in Jesus name, Amen.

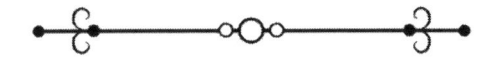

Jesus' Teaching on Prayer

Luke 11:1-13

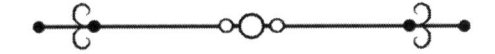

When he finished praying in a certain place, one of his disciples said to him, "Lord, teach us to pray, just as John also taught his disciples."

He said to them, "When you pray, say,

'Our Father in heaven,
may your name be kept holy.
May your Kingdom come.
May your will be done on earth, as it is in heaven.
Give us day by day our daily bread.
Forgive us our sins,
for we ourselves also forgive everyone who is indebted to us.
Bring us not into temptation,
but deliver us from the evil one.'"

He said to them, "Which of you, if you go to a friend at midnight, and tell him, 'Friend, lend me three loaves of bread, for a friend of mine has come to me from a journey, and I have nothing to set before him,' and he from within will answer and say, 'Don't bother me.

The door is now shut, and my children are with me in bed. I can't get up and give it to you'? I tell you, although he will not rise and give it to him because he is his friend, yet because of his persistence, he will get up and give him as many as he needs.

"I tell you, keep asking, and it will be given you. Keep seeking, and you will find. Keep knocking, and it will be opened to you. For everyone who asks receives. He who seeks finds. To him who knocks it will be opened.

"Which of you fathers, if your son asks for bread, will give him a stone? Or if he asks for a fish, he won't give him a snake instead of a fish, will he? Or if he asks for an egg, he won't give him a scorpion, will he?

If you then, being evil, know how to give good gifts to your children, how much more will your heavenly Father give the Holy Spirit to those who ask him?"

Father, your heart is to bless, to guide, to answer prayer and to give us good things. How often I forget to ask and instead take matters into my own hands. How often I turn to others for good things instead of turning to you. Forgive me Lord. I love you so much. I pray that my testimony will be of asking and being answered, seeking and finding, and knocking and seeing doors opened. I want you to be glorified in my life. I know that by forgetting to ask you to provide or make a way, I am missing the opportunity to seeing prayers answered. Lord Jesus, you answered every question that was put to you. You taught us how to live, you taught us about friendship and you taught us having a relationship with the Father. I cannot put into words how much you mean to me, and how unfathomable I find your love.

Jesus and Beelzebub

Luke 11:14-28

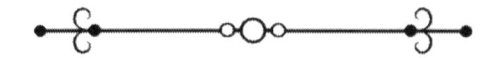

He was casting out a demon, and it was mute. When the demon had gone out, the mute man spoke; and the multitudes marvelled. But some of them said, "He casts out demons by Beelzebul, the prince of the demons." Others, testing him, sought from him a sign from heaven. But he, knowing their thoughts, said to them, "Every kingdom divided against itself is brought to desolation. A house divided against itself falls. If Satan also is divided against himself, how will his kingdom stand? For you say that I cast out demons by Beelzebul. But if I cast out demons by Beelzebul, by whom do your children cast them out? Therefore they will be your judges. But if I by God's finger cast out demons, then God's Kingdom has come to you.

"When the strong man, fully armed, guards his own dwelling, his goods are safe. But when someone stronger attacks him and overcomes him, he takes from him his whole armour in which he trusted, and divides his plunder.

"He that is not with me is against me. He who doesn't gather with me scatters. The unclean spirit, when he has gone out of the man, passes through dry places, seeking rest, and finding none, he says, 'I will turn back to my house from which I came out.' When he returns, he finds it swept and put in order. Then he goes, and takes seven other spirits more evil than himself, and they enter in and dwell there. The last state of that man becomes worse than the first."

It came to pass, as he said these things, a certain woman out of the multitude lifted up her voice, and said to him, "Blessed is the womb that bore you, and the breasts which nursed you!"

But he said, "On the contrary, blessed are those who hear the word of God, and keep it."

∞∞◯∞∞

"Blessed rather are those who hear the word of God and obey it." This is what I want in my life. I want my life to be a reflection of your word. Help me to understand the Bible. Help me to apply it to my life. Help me to know you more as I read it. Fill me with your Spirit Lord and change me to be more like you. Please let me bring you honour and glory. Please give me opportunity to tell those around me what it is that you have done. I find it so difficult to speak effectively about you. I need you to guide me and help me with my speech. I am willing O God. Help me to hear and to obey. In Jesus name I pray, Amen.

THE SIGN OF JONAH

LUKE 11:29-32

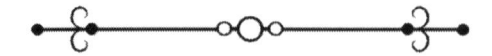

When the multitudes were gathering together to him, he began to say, "This is an evil generation. It seeks after a sign. No sign will be given to it but the sign of Jonah, the prophet. For even as Jonah became a sign to the Ninevites, so will also the Son of Man be to this generation. The Queen of the South will rise up in the judgment with the men of this generation, and will condemn them: for she came from the ends of the earth to hear the wisdom of Solomon; and behold, one greater than Solomon is here. The men of Nineveh will stand up in the judgment with this generation, and will condemn it: for they repented at the preaching of Jonah, and behold, one greater than Jonah is here.

Lord God, I pray for repentant hearts in my generation. I pray that you will soften hearts in my city. I ask you that the good news of the death and resurrection of your Son become the life and hope of my friends and neighbours. I pray you will pour your Spirit out,

O God. Have mercy and reach out your hand to save. I pray for believers full of zeal for your name. Let us be full of courage and boldness in declaring your word. I pray for hearts that will turn away from evil and sin and receive your Son. In Jesus name I pray, Amen.

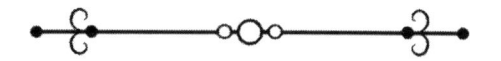

THE LAMP OF THE BODY

LUKE 11:33-36

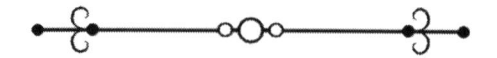

"No one, when he has lit a lamp, puts it in a cellar or under a basket, but on a stand, that those who come in may see the light. The lamp of the body is the eye. Therefore when your eye is good, your whole body is also full of light; but when it is evil, your body also is full of darkness. Therefore see whether the light that is in you isn't darkness. If therefore your whole body is full of light, having no part dark, it will be wholly full of light, as when the lamp with its bright shining gives you light."

O God, let your name be lifted up above all other names. Let the wonder of your creation bring people to their knees in awe of your majesty. Let every believer allow your work in their life so that you might be glorified. I pray this in my own life. Make me aware of opportunities to lift up your name in praise. Let my heart be full of thanksgiving and blessings for the things you have done. Let my life be filled with the light and glory of your Son. Be glorified my Lord and my God, Amen.

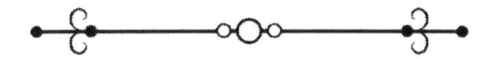

SIX WOES

LUKE 11:37-54

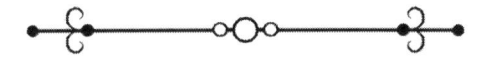

Now as he spoke, a certain Pharisee asked him to dine with him. He went in, and sat at the table. When the Pharisee saw it, he marvelled that he had not first washed himself before dinner.

The Lord said to him, "Now you Pharisees cleanse the outside of the cup and of the platter, but your inward part is full of extortion and wickedness. You foolish ones, didn't he who made the outside make the inside also? But give for gifts to the needy those things which are within, and behold, all things will be clean to you. But woe to you Pharisees! For you tithe mint and rue and every herb, but you bypass justice and God's love. You ought to have done these, and not to have left the other undone.

Woe to you Pharisees! For you love the best seats in the synagogues, and the greetings in the marketplaces. Woe to you, scribes and Pharisees, hypocrites! For you are like hidden graves, and the men who walk over them don't know it."

One of the lawyers answered him, "Teacher, in saying this you insult us also."

He said, "Woe to you lawyers also! For you load men with burdens that are difficult to carry, and you yourselves won't even lift one finger to help carry those burdens. Woe to you! For you build the tombs of the prophets, and your fathers killed them. So you testify and consent to the works of your fathers. For they killed them, and you build their tombs. Therefore also the wisdom of God said, 'I will send to them prophets and apostles; and some of them they will kill and persecute, that the blood of all the prophets, which was shed from the foundation of the world, may be required of this generation; from the blood of Abel to the blood of Zachariah, who perished between the altar and the sanctuary.' Yes, I tell you, it will be required of this generation. Woe to you lawyers! For you took away the key of knowledge. You didn't enter in yourselves, and those who were entering in, you hindered."

As he said these things to them, the scribes and the Pharisees began to be terribly angry, and to draw many things out of him; lying in wait for him, and seeking to catch him in something he might say, that they might accuse him.

Father, I don't want hypocrisy in my life. I don't want to appear to be something on the surface, yet inside be something completely different. Father, cleanse my heart. Forgive my sin. I pray for grace and wisdom to bring blessing on your name. I ask that you will work within me and root out anything ugly and false in my life. I want your truth to shine out of my life and I want nothing to do with anything else. No matter how difficult it is, please show me if I need to deal with any double standards I might have. Let my life shine forth your truth and love, in Jesus name I pray, Amen.

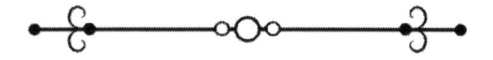

WARNINGS AND ENCOURAGEMENTS

LUKE 12:1-12

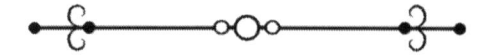

Meanwhile, when a multitude of many thousands had gathered together, so much so that they trampled on each other, he began to tell his disciples first of all, "Beware of the yeast of the Pharisees, which is hypocrisy. But there is nothing covered up, that will not be revealed, nor hidden, that will not be known. Therefore whatever you have said in the darkness will be heard in the light. What you have spoken in the ear in the inner rooms will be proclaimed on the housetops.

"I tell you, my friends, don't be afraid of those who kill the body, and after that have no more that they can do. But I will warn you whom you should fear. Fear him, who after he has killed, has power to cast into Gehenna. Yes, I tell you, fear him.

"Aren't five sparrows sold for two assaria coins? Not one of them is forgotten by God. But the very hairs of your head are all counted. Therefore don't be afraid. You are of more value than many sparrows.

"I tell you, everyone who confesses me before men, him will the Son of Man also confess before the angels of God; but he who denies me in the presence of men will be denied in the presence of the angels of God. Everyone who speaks a word against the Son of Man will be forgiven, but those who blaspheme against the Holy Spirit will not be forgiven. When they bring you before the synagogues, the rulers, and the authorities, don't be anxious how or what you will answer, or what you will say; for the Holy Spirit will teach you in that same hour what you must say."

Lord I don't understand why you are concerned for mankind. I don't understand how you can care for each one of us to the extent of knowing the number of hairs on our heads. I cannot comprehend how you know the life of each sparrow and everything that goes on in creation, and at the same time hold my life, my family my friends and my future in your hands. I cannot grasp how it is that I can be of any significance to you whatsoever, but I know that I am. I know that your word is clear that I belong to you, and you have promised to take care of me, whether I understand why or not. Thank you Lord God for your loving-kindness towards me. Thank you for your concern and involvement in my life. Thank you that you direct my paths and help me walk in them. I love you Lord, Amen.

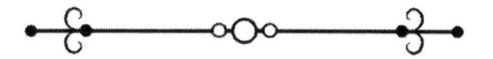

THE PARABLE OF THE RICH FOOL

LUKE 12:13-21

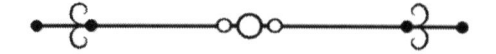

One of the multitude said to him, "Teacher, tell my brother to divide the inheritance with me."

But he said to him, "Man, who made me a judge or an arbitrator over you?" He said to them, "Beware! Keep yourselves from covetousness, for a man's life doesn't consist of the abundance of the things which he possesses."

He spoke a parable to them, saying, "The ground of a certain rich man produced abundantly. He reasoned within himself, saying, 'What will I do, because I don't have room to store my crops?' He said, 'This is what I will do. I will pull down my barns, and build bigger ones, and there I will store all my grain and my goods. I will tell my soul, "Soul, you have many goods laid up for many years. Take your ease, eat, drink, be merry."'

"But God said to him, 'You foolish one, tonight your soul is required of you. The things which you have *prepared—whose will they be?' So is he who lays up treasure for himself, and is not rich toward God."*

⸻

Father, I know that I can make plans in my life, but it is you that directs my path. I know that I have often made plans and you have directed me in a different direction. Lord, I trust you with my life. I trust you with my future. I pray that I won't take my eyes off you when I make decisions. I pray indeed that you will be a part of every decision I make. I want you to direct my paths. I don't want to go off and insist on my own way. Please guard my heart that I might not work for 'things' instead of remembering that this life is temporary. In Jesus name I pray, Amen.

DO NOT WORRY

LUKE 12:22:34

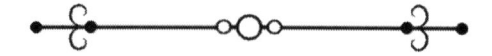

He said to his disciples, "Therefore I tell you, don't be anxious for your life, what you will eat, nor yet for your body, what you will wear. Life is more than food, and the body is more than clothing. Consider the ravens: they don't sow, they don't reap, they have no warehouse or barn, and God feeds them. How much more valuable are you than birds!

Which of you by being anxious can add a cubit to his height? If then you aren't able to do even the least things, why are you anxious about the rest? Consider the lilies, how they grow. They don't toil, neither do they spin; yet I tell you, even Solomon in all his glory was not arrayed like one of these. But if this is how God clothes the grass in the field, which today exists, and tomorrow is cast into the oven, how much more will he clothe you, O you of little faith?

Don't seek what you will eat or what you will drink; neither be anxious. For the nations of the world seek after all of these things, but your Father knows that you need these things. But seek God's Kingdom, and all these things will be added to you. Don't be afraid, little flock, for it is your Father's good pleasure to give you the Kingdom. Sell that which you have, and give gifts to the needy. Make for yourselves purses which don't grow old, a treasure in the heavens that doesn't fail, where no thief approaches, neither moth destroys. For where your treasure is, there will your heart be also.

ooo◯ooo

Lord, you are my treasure. You are my foundation and my strength. All wisdom and grace for living a life centred around you, comes from you. Thank you for your loving-kindness. Thank you that you look after me. My every need is provided and I lack nothing. I pray that you will continue to work in my life. I ask that you continue to mould my heart to be more like Jesus. I ask you to forgive me for the times that I haven't trusted you and taken matters into my own hands. Forgive me for the times where I worry about things instead of turning to you. There is no-one like you. No-one who promises what you promise, and no-one who fulfils their promises like you. Amen.

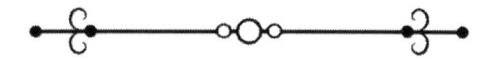

WATCHFULNESS

LUKE 12:35-48

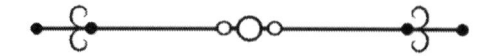

"Let your waist be dressed and your lamps burning. Be like men watching for their lord, when he returns from the marriage feast; that, when he comes and knocks, they may immediately open to him. Blessed are those servants, whom the lord will find watching when he comes. Most certainly I tell you, that he will dress himself, and make them recline, and will come and serve them. They will be blessed if he comes in the second or third watch, and finds them so. But know this, that if the master of the house had known in what hour the thief was coming, he would have watched, and not allowed his house to be broken into. Therefore be ready also, for the Son of Man is coming in an hour that you don't expect him."

Peter said to him, "Lord, are you telling this parable to us, or to everybody?"

The Lord said, "Who then is the faithful and wise steward, whom his lord will set over his household, to give them their portion of food at the right times?

Blessed is that servant whom his lord will find doing so when he comes. Truly I tell you, that he will set him over all that he has. But if that servant says in his heart, 'My lord delays his coming,' and begins to beat the menservants and the maidservants, and to eat and drink, and to be drunken, then the lord of that servant will come in a day when he isn't expecting him, and in an hour that he doesn't know, and will cut him in two, and place his portion with the unfaithful. That servant, who knew his lord's will, and didn't prepare, nor do what he wanted, will be beaten with many stripes, but he who didn't know, and did things worthy of stripes, will be beaten with few stripes. To whomever much is given, of him will much be required; and to whom much was entrusted, of him more will be asked.

○○○○⬤○○○○

Lord Jesus, I want to be like those servants who were ready for their master when you come. I want my life to be faithful and true to you no matter what the circumstances. Please help me in my worldliness and my struggle against sin. Help me overcome and keep my eyes firmly fixed on you. I pray you will guard my heart against apathy and unbelief. Lord, I long to hear those words 'Well done, good and faithful servant.' I long to see your face and be in your presence forever; but whilst I am here on earth, I pray you will give me a steadfast heart and wisdom to know your will. I ask this in your name, Amen.

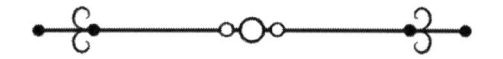

NOT PEACE BUT DIVISION

LUKE 12:49-53

"I came to throw fire on the earth. I wish it were already kindled. But I have a baptism to be baptized with, and how distressed I am until it is accomplished!

Do you think that I have come to give peace in the earth? I tell you, no, but rather division. For from now on, there will be five in one house divided, three against two, and two against three.

They will be divided, father against son, and son against father; mother against daughter, and daughter against her mother; mother-in-law against her daughter-in-law, and daughter-in-law against her mother-in-law."

Father I pray for those who love you and who stand alone in their families as believers. I pray that you will strengthen them and fill them with your Holy Spirit so that they might persevere in their faith. Draw them close to you and give them comfort as they struggle with their families. I pray that your light might shine through them and draw those unbelieving members to you, in Jesus name I pray, Amen.

INTERPRETING THE TIMES

LUKE 12:54-59

He said to the multitudes also, "When you see a cloud rising from the west, immediately you say, 'A shower is coming,' and so it happens. When a south wind blows, you say, 'There will be a scorching heat,' and it happens. You hypocrites! You know how to interpret the appearance of the earth and the sky, but how is it that you don't interpret this time? Why don't you judge for yourselves what is right? For when you are going with your adversary before the magistrate, try diligently on the way to be released from him, lest perhaps he drag you to the judge, and the judge deliver you to the officer, and the officer throw you into prison. I tell you, you will by no means get out of there, until you have paid the very last penny."

Lord Jesus, whilst you were here on earth, men did not recognise you as Messiah. You healed, you cast out demons, you did miracle after miracle and instead of recognising you and believing in you, many turned their backs and refused to believe the evidence before them. They did not see the clear signs that their God walked among them. I pray that you will give me wisdom and discernment to follow you. Soften my heart and make me sensitive to your voice. I desire above all things to serve and honour you. I ask you to forgive me for those times, when I, like those who saw you in the flesh, doubted and disbelieved things that came from you. Help me to recognise your hand at work in my life. Help me to serve you according to your will. I ask this in your holy name, Amen.

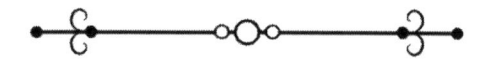

REPENT OR PERISH

LUKE 13:1-9

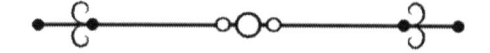

Now there were some present at the same time who told him about the Galileans, whose blood Pilate had mixed with their sacrifices. Jesus answered them, "Do you think that these Galileans were worse sinners than all the other Galileans, because they suffered such things? I tell you, no, but unless you repent, you will all perish in the same way. Or those eighteen, on whom the tower in Siloam fell, and killed them; do you think that they were worse offenders than all the men who dwell in Jerusalem? I tell you, no, but, unless you repent, you will all perish in the same way."

He spoke this parable. "A certain man had a fig tree planted in his vineyard, and he came seeking fruit on it, and found none. He said to the vine dresser, 'Behold, these three years I have come looking for fruit on this fig tree, and found none. Cut it down. Why does it waste the soil?' He answered, 'Lord, leave it alone this year also, until I dig around it, and fertilize it. If it bears fruit, fine; but if not, after that, you can cut it down.'"

○○○‧○‧○○○

Lord God, I pray that my life would be one that brings forth fruit in keeping with my relationship with you. Please help me to see the opportunities you put before me. Give me compassion and a heart of kindness so that you are glorified in my life. I know that unless you give me the desire to obey you, it is impossible for me to do so. You promised that you would give us the will to do your good purpose. This is what I want in my life. I want my family and friends around me to be blessed. I want by my very life, to bring honour to your name. I want your purposes to be worked out in my life. I ask this in Jesus name, Amen.

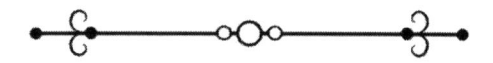

A Crippled Woman Healed on the Sabbath

Luke 13:10-17

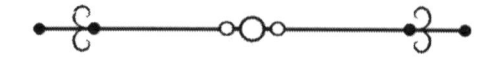

He was teaching in one of the synagogues on the Sabbath day. Behold, there was a woman who had a spirit of infirmity eighteen years, and she was bent over, and could in no way straighten herself up. When Jesus saw her, he called her, and said to her, "Woman, you are freed from your infirmity." He laid his hands on her, and immediately she stood up straight, and glorified God.

The ruler of the synagogue, being indignant because Jesus had healed on the Sabbath, said to the multitude, "There are six days in which men ought to work. Therefore come on those days and be healed, and not on the Sabbath day!"

Therefore the Lord answered him, "You hypocrites! Doesn't each one of you free his ox or his donkey from the stall on the Sabbath, and lead him away to water? Ought not this woman, being a daughter of Abraham, *whom Satan had bound eighteen long years, be freed from this bondage on the Sabbath day?"*

As he said these things, all his adversaries were disappointed, and all the multitude rejoiced for all the glorious things that were done by him.

<hr>

Lord Jesus, you delight to heal. You delight to deliver. Your compassion for those who are in pain and suffering is unending. You are my Saviour and Lord and I love you. Thank you for your work in my life. Thank you that you did not just save me, but you continue to carry on your work in my life, changing me to be more like you every day. Root out every hypocritical attitude in me. I want no part in it. Holy Spirit, fill me that I might bring glory to the Father. Fill me that I might hear your voice and obey. Fill me that I might bless those around me, in Jesus name I pray, Amen.

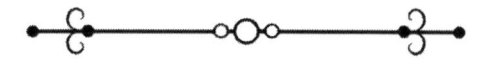

THE PARABLES OF THE MUSTARD SEED AND THE YEAST

LUKE 13:18-21

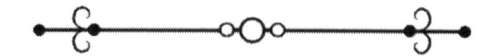

He said, "What is God's Kingdom like? To what shall I compare it? It is like a grain of mustard seed, which a man took, and put in his own garden. It grew, and became a large tree, and the birds of the sky live in its branches."

Again he said, "To what shall I compare God's Kingdom? It is like yeast, which a woman took and hid in three measures of flour, until it was all leavened."

Lord God, your kingdom has grown from one man, to encompass every nation. Your word has saved the lives of countless millions. You are a God of mercy and compassion. You draw near to all who call on your name and fulfil the desire of all who love you. You hear every prayer and you answer. You watch over all who love you and you direct their paths.

Let your kingdom come Lord. Let your kingdom come in my life. Let your kingdom come in my family and friends. Let your kingdom come in my neighbourhood and town. O God, let the people see your glory and be saved, in Jesus holy name I pray, Amen.

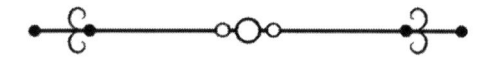

THE NARROW DOOR

LUKE 13:22-30

He went on his way through cities and villages, teaching, and travelling on to Jerusalem. One said to him, "Lord, are they few who are saved?"

He said to them, "Strive to enter in by the narrow door, for many, I tell you, will seek to enter in, and will not be able. When once the master of the house has risen up, and has shut the door, and you begin to stand outside, and to knock at the door, saying, 'Lord, Lord, open to us!' then he will answer and tell you, 'I don't know you or where you come from.' Then you will begin to say, 'We ate and drank in your presence, and you taught in our streets.' He will say, 'I tell you, I don't know where you come from. Depart from me, all you workers of iniquity.' There will be weeping and gnashing of teeth, when you see Abraham, Isaac, Jacob, and all the prophets, in God's Kingdom, and yourselves being thrown outside. They will come from the east, west, north, and south, and will sit down in God's Kingdom. Behold, there are some who are last who will be first, and there are some who are first who will be last."

∞∞⦿∞∞

Father, please help me to keep my eyes fixed on you. Help me to read the Bible every day so I might draw close to you. I do not want to be led astray by strange teaching, or something appealing that might sound right, but isn't. Please protect me from the plans of Satan. I want to draw close to you and never leave your side. O God, work in my life. Forgive my faithlessness and lack of wisdom. Forgive my apathy and lack of consistence when it comes to my walk with you. I hate this. I want to be found faithful, and yet I look at my Christian walk all I see is a cycle of faithfulness and apathy. I want to be faithful all the time. I am fed up of always seeing this cycle in my life. Please work in me. Please change my heart. I love you so much Lord and I don't know why this keeps happening. Mould me to be more like you. Fill me with your Spirit. Fill me with your power so that I might live a life that brings you glory, in Jesus name I pray, Amen.

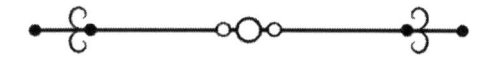

Jesus' Sorrow for Jerusalem

Luke 13:31-35

On that same day, some Pharisees came, saying to him, "Get out of here, and go away, for Herod wants to kill you."

He said to them, "Go and tell that fox, 'Behold, I cast out demons and perform cures today and tomorrow, and the third day I complete my mission. Nevertheless I must go on my way today and tomorrow and the next day, for it can't be that a prophet would perish outside of Jerusalem.'

"Jerusalem, Jerusalem, that kills the prophets, and stones those who are sent to her! How often I wanted to gather your children together, like a hen gathers her own brood under her wings, and you refused! Behold, your house is left to you desolate. I tell you, you will not see me, until you say, 'Blessed is he who comes in the name of the Lord!'"

Lord Jesus, as I read these scriptures I see your complete resolve to do your Father's will. You did not fear man, and what he could do to you. You had complete trust that no-one could do anything to you, unless it was allowed by God. I thank you that this is true in my life too. Thank you that there is nothing beyond your control. My children are in your hands. My husband is in your hands. Indeed the direction of my life is in your hands. Thank you for this security I have in you. I don't need to fear tomorrow as I know nothing will befall me that you have not allowed. I know that no matter what happens, you are with me. Thank you Lord, Amen.

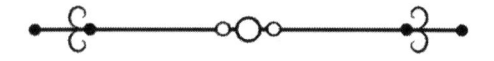

Jesus at a Pharisee's House

Luke 14:1-14

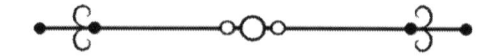

When he went into the house of one of the rulers of the Pharisees on a Sabbath to eat bread, they were watching him. Behold, a certain man who had dropsy was in front of him. Jesus, answering, spoke to the lawyers and Pharisees, saying, "Is it lawful to heal on the Sabbath?"

But they were silent.

He took him, and healed him, and let him go. He answered them, "Which of you, if your son or an ox fell into a well, wouldn't immediately pull him out on a Sabbath day?"

They couldn't answer him regarding these things.

He spoke a parable to those who were invited, when he noticed how they chose the best seats, and said to them, "When you are invited by anyone to a marriage feast, don't sit in the best seat, since perhaps someone more honourable than you might be invited by him, and he who invited both of you would come and tell you, 'Make room for this person.' Then you would begin, with shame, to take the lowest place. But when you are invited, go and sit in the lowest place, so that when he who invited you comes, he may tell you, 'Friend, move up higher.' Then you will be honoured in the presence of all who sit at the table with you. For everyone who exalts himself will be humbled, and whoever humbles himself will be exalted."

He also said to the one who had invited him, "When you make a dinner or a supper, don't call your friends, nor your brothers, nor your kinsmen, nor rich neighbours, or perhaps they might also return the favour, and pay you back. But when you make a feast, ask the poor, the maimed, the lame, or the blind; and you will be blessed, because they don't have the resources to repay you. For you will be repaid in the resurrection of the righteous."

∞∞◯∞∞

Create in me a clean heart O God, and renew a right spirit within me. There is none like you Lord God. None who can take a filthy heart full of sin and change it to one that is pure and clean. I was once dead in sin, but now, because of your great mercy and love, I am alive in Christ. You have not just given me life, but you have given me hope and you are changing me. Forgive me for the many times I have done things for the good opinion of other people, instead of asking your opinion. Forgive me for when I have been proud and considered myself first, instead of those around me. Thank you for your forgiveness. Thank you for cleansing my heart. Thank you for your amazing grace. Amen.

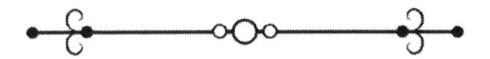

The Parable of the Great Banquet

Luke 14:15-24

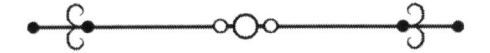

When one of those who sat at the table with him heard these things, he said to him, "Blessed is he who will feast in God's Kingdom!"

But he said to him, "A certain man made a great supper, and he invited many people. He sent out his servant at supper time to tell those who were invited, 'Come, for everything is ready now.' They all as one began to make excuses.

"The first said to him, 'I have bought a field, and I must go and see it. Please have me excused.'

"Another said, 'I have bought five yoke of oxen, and I must go try them out. Please have me excused.'

"Another said, 'I have married a wife, and therefore I can't come.'

"That servant came, and told his lord these things. Then the master of the house, being angry, said to his servant, 'Go out quickly into the streets and lanes of

the city, and bring in the poor, maimed, blind, and lame.'

"The servant said, 'Lord, it is done as you commanded, and there is still room.'

"The lord said to the servant, 'Go out into the highways and hedges, and compel them to come in, that my house may be filled. For I tell you that none of those men who were invited will taste of my supper.'"

∞∞○∞∞

Thank you Lord that my destiny is to eat at the feast in your kingdom. I am longing for that day to arrive. I pray that whilst I am here on earth you will use me to tell those around me about your great mercy. Please give me opportunity to share about what Jesus did on the cross and what a difference life is when there is such hope and such a wonderful future with you. Please give me insight and wisdom to understand the gospel more. Give me the ability to put it into words so that people might understand. Lord I am your servant. I am willing to go and tell people about you. Please give me opportunity and courage, in Jesus name I pray, Amen.

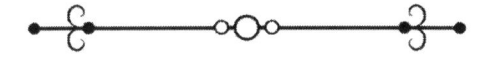

The Cost of Being a Disciple

Luke 14:25-35

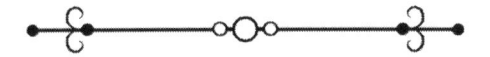

Now great multitudes were going with him. He turned and said to them, "If anyone comes to me, and doesn't disregard his own father, mother, wife, children, brothers, and sisters, yes, and his own life also, he can't be my disciple. Whoever doesn't bear his own cross, and come after me, can't be my disciple. For which of you, desiring to build a tower, doesn't first sit down and count the cost, to see if he has enough to complete it? Or perhaps, when he has laid a foundation, and is not able to finish, everyone who sees begins to mock him, saying, 'This man began to build, and wasn't able to finish.' Or what king, as he goes to encounter another king in war, will not sit down first and consider whether he is able with ten thousand to meet him who comes against him with twenty thousand? Or else, while the other is yet a great way off, he sends an envoy, and asks for conditions of peace. So therefore whoever of you who doesn't renounce all that he has, he can't be my disciple. Salt is good, but if the salt becomes flat and

tasteless, with what do you season it? It is fit neither for the soil nor for the manure pile. It is thrown out. He who has ears to hear, let him hear."

○○○−○−○○○

You are my Lord and my God. I will follow you wherever you lead me. I have counted the cost and want my whole life to be dedicated to bringing you glory and honour. Guard me against becoming apathetic and uncaring. Fill my life with faith that I might walk on the path you have chosen for me. I have considered and thought about my life, and I want it to be fully lived in your service. Everything is meaningless without you. No job, or friendship, or adventure has any worth outside of your love. You give my life purpose and I love that you care so much for me that no detail of my life is hidden from you. I love that you guide me and I am not alone. I wish I could put into words how much I love you. Amen.

THE PARABLE OF THE LOST SHEEP

LUKE 15:1-7

Now all the tax collectors and sinners were coming close to him to hear him. The Pharisees and the scribes murmured, saying, "This man welcomes sinners, and eats with them."

He told them this parable. "Which of you men, if you had one hundred sheep, and lost one of them, wouldn't leave the ninety-nine in the wilderness, and go after the one that was lost, until he found it? When he has found it, he carries it on his shoulders, rejoicing. When he comes home, he calls together his friends and his neighbours, saying to them, 'Rejoice with me, for I have found my sheep which was lost!' I tell you that even so there will be more joy in heaven over one sinner who repents, than over ninety-nine righteous people who need no repentance.

O God, I pray that I will never be too proud to befriend people whom others might despise. I ask you for grace in those situations to truly care for their needs and to bless them. Help me to be willing to go the extra mile and to make time for people in need. Lead me to 'lost sheep' Lord and use me to bring them back to you. Change my heart to be compassionate and full of grace, so I might show your love in every situation. In Jesus name I pray, Amen.

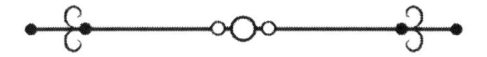

The Parable of the Lost Coin

Luke 15:8-10

Or what woman, if she had ten drachma coins, if she lost one drachma coin, wouldn't light a lamp, sweep the house, and seek diligently until she found it? When she has found it, she calls together her friends and neighbours, saying, 'Rejoice with me, for I have found the drachma which I had lost.' Even so, I tell you, there is joy in the presence of the angels of God over one sinner repenting."

You Lord God reached out to mankind and made a way for me to have a relationship with you. You sent your Son to die an agonizing death and bear the punishment for my sin so that I might have eternal life. Without your first drawing me to you, and causing your Spirit to work in my heart, I would never have had the desire to turn to you in the first place, let alone commit my life into your hands. All the work was done by you. ALL of it. Your Word says angels rejoice when a sinner repents. Angels rejoiced on the day I turned away from my old life and gave it to you. They rejoiced at yet another display of your grace and mercy at work. I cannot comprehend the depths of your love. All I can say is, *thank you*. Thank you for not leaving me to muddle through life on my own. Thank you for giving me a future in your kingdom and not having to face an eternity of hell. Who is there like you, O God? Amen.

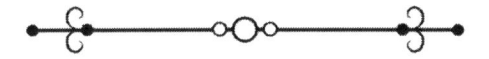

THE PARABLE OF THE LOST SON

LUKE 15:11-24

He said, "A certain man had two sons. The younger of them said to his father, 'Father, give me my share of your property.' He divided his livelihood between them. Not many days after, the younger son gathered all of this together and travelled into a far country. There he wasted his property with riotous living. When he had spent all of it, there arose a severe famine in that country, and he began to be in need. He went and joined himself to one of the citizens of that country, and he sent him into his fields to feed pigs. He wanted to fill his belly with the husks that the pigs ate, but no one gave him any.

But when he came to himself he said, 'How many hired servants of my father's have bread enough to spare, and I'm dying with hunger! I will get up and go to my father, and will tell him, "Father, I have sinned against heaven, and in your sight. I am no more worthy to be called your son. Make me as one of your hired servants."'

"He arose, and came to his father. But while he was still far off, his father saw him, and was moved with compassion, and ran, and fell on his neck, and kissed him. The son said to him, 'Father, I have sinned against heaven, and in your sight. I am no longer worthy to be called your son.'

"But the father said to his servants, 'Bring out the best robe, and put it on him. Put a ring on his hand, and shoes on his feet. Bring the fattened calf, kill it, and let's eat, and celebrate; for this, my son, was dead, and is alive again. He was lost, and is found.' They began to celebrate.

◦◦◦○◦◦◦

It is incredible to me that I can call you Father. You took me, gave me life, adopted me and have given me a future in your kingdom. There are no words to express your incredible undeserved favour. Saying 'thank you' just doesn't seem enough. Even so, all I can say is 'thank you' my Lord for having mercy on me and accepting me as your child. I know that I don't deserve it. Thank you. May my life constantly point others to you that they too might experience this amazing grace, in Jesus name I ask, Amen.

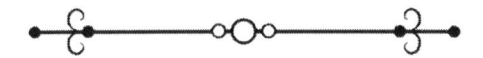

The Older Brother
Luke 15:25-32

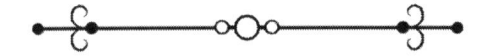

"Now his elder son was in the field. As he came near to the house, he heard music and dancing. He called one of the servants to him, and asked what was going on. He said to him, 'Your brother has come, and your father has killed the fattened calf, because he has received him back safe and healthy.' But he was angry, and would not go in. Therefore his father came out, and begged him. But he answered his father, 'Behold, these many years I have served you, and I never disobeyed a commandment of yours, but you never gave me a goat, that I might celebrate with my friends. But when this your son came, who has devoured your living with prostitutes, you killed the fattened calf for him.'

"He said to him, 'Son, you are always with me, and all that is mine is yours. But it was appropriate to celebrate and be glad, for this, your brother, was dead, and is alive again. He was lost, and is found.'"

I ask you Lord that I might never forget that you have accepted me as your child. I ask that I will never turn away and behave as if I need to earn your love. I know that you have freely accepted me, freely forgiven me and freely given me new life. Please help me live daily in the knowledge of this freedom. Let me never be tempted to put on the chains of serving you for a reward. Please give me words to share this freedom with my family and friends. I see them so bound in the cares of this life and I long to see them blessed by your presence and experiencing your forgiveness. Please stretch out your arm to save, for your name's sake, Amen.

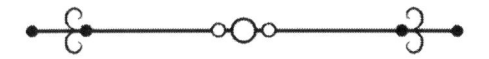

THE PARABLE OF THE SHREWD MANAGER

LUKE 16:1-15

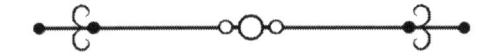

He also said to his disciples, "There was a certain rich man who had a manager. An accusation was made to him that this man was wasting his possessions. He called him, and said to him, 'What is this that I hear about you? Give an accounting of your management, for you can no longer be manager.'

"The manager said within himself, 'What will I do, seeing that my lord is taking away the management position from me? I don't have strength to dig. I am ashamed to beg. I know what I will do, so that when I am removed from management, they may receive me into their houses.'

Calling each one of his lord's debtors to him, he said to the first, 'How much do you owe to my lord?' He said, 'A hundred batos of oil.' He said to him, 'Take your bill, and sit down quickly and write fifty.' Then he said to another, 'How much do you owe?' He said, 'A hundred cors of wheat.' He said to him, 'Take your bill, and write eighty.'

"His lord commended the dishonest manager because he had done wisely, for the children of this world are, in their own generation, wiser than the children of the light. I tell you, make for yourselves friends by means of unrighteous mammon, so that when you fail, they may receive you into the eternal tents.

He who is faithful in a very little is faithful also in much. He who is dishonest in a very little is also dishonest in much. If therefore you have not been faithful in the unrighteous mammon, who will commit to your trust the true riches? If you have not been faithful in that which is another's, who will give you that which is your own?

No servant can serve two masters, for either he will hate the one, and love the other; or else he will hold to one, and despise the other. You aren't able to serve God and Mammon."

The Pharisees, who were lovers of money, also heard all these things, and they scoffed at him. He said to them, "You are those who justify yourselves in the sight of men, but God knows your hearts. For that which is exalted among men is an abomination in the sight of God.

○○○-○-○○○

Lord I ask forgiveness for the times when something small has been asked of me and I have not helped out, whether from laziness or disinterest. Please change my heart that I might care deeply for those around me. Lift me out of this apathy that holds me at times so strongly that I feel I can't do anything. I want to be faithful in my service to you. I want my every action to bring glory to your name. O God, you are the only one who can change my heart. I am willing O Lord, please change me, make me into the image of your Son, so that my life will constantly point to you. I ask in Jesus name, Amen.

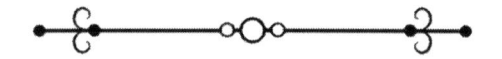

ADDITIONAL TEACHINGS

LUKE 16:16-18

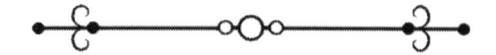

The law and the prophets were until John. From that time the Good News of God's Kingdom is preached, and everyone is forcing his way into it. But it is easier for heaven and earth to pass away, than for one tiny stroke of a pen in the law to fall. Everyone who divorces his wife, and marries another, commits adultery. He who marries one who is divorced from a husband commits adultery.

How great is your word O Lord my God. In you there is wisdom and knowledge. In you can be found the answer to any question of life. In you there is light and life. Wherever your word is taught, lives change. Wherever your word is heard, hearts are moulded. Your word is true, perfect and eternal. It is living and active, no-one who hears your word comes away the same. Blessed be your holy name. Amen.

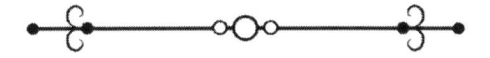

THE RICH MAN AND LAZARUS
LUKE 16:19-31

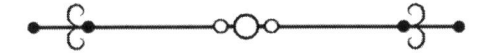

"Now there was a certain rich man, and he was clothed in purple and fine linen, living in luxury every day. A certain beggar, named Lazarus, was taken to his gate, full of sores, and desiring to be fed with the crumbs that fell from the rich man's table. Yes, even the dogs came and licked his sores. The beggar died, and he was carried away by the angels to Abraham's bosom. The rich man also died, and was buried. In Hades, he lifted up his eyes, being in torment, and saw Abraham far off, and Lazarus at his bosom. He cried and said, 'Father Abraham, have mercy on me, and send Lazarus, that he may dip the tip of his finger in water, and cool my tongue! For I am in anguish in this flame.'

"But Abraham said, 'Son, remember that you, in your lifetime, received your good things, and Lazarus, in the same way, bad things. But here he is now comforted, and you are in anguish. Besides all this, between us and you there is a great gulf fixed, that

those who want to pass from here to you are not able, and that no one may cross over from there to us.'

"He said, 'I ask you therefore, father, that you would send him to my father's house; for I have five brothers, that he may testify to them, so they won't also come into this place of torment.'

"But Abraham said to him, 'They have Moses and the prophets. Let them listen to them.'

"He said, 'No, father Abraham, but if one goes to them from the dead, they will repent.'

"He said to him, 'If they don't listen to Moses and the prophets, neither will they be persuaded if one rises from the dead.'"

◦◦◦◦○◦◦◦◦

Father, please forgive me when I have been proud like the rich man in this parable. I know at times I am arrogant and self-righteous. I don't want this in my life. I know you have given me undeserved favour and there is no place for self importance. Please make a way with my family and friends that I might be able to tell them about you and what you have done. Could you prepare their hearts, so that the gospel might find ground to grow and flourish? O God, please save my family. Save my friends. Have mercy on them and give them life. I ask this in Jesus name, Amen.

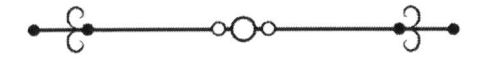

Sin Faith, Duty

Luke 17:1-10

He said to the disciples, "It is impossible that no occasions of stumbling should come, but woe to him through whom they come! It would be better for him if a millstone were hung around his neck, and he were thrown into the sea, rather than that he should cause one of these little ones to stumble. Be careful. If your brother sins against you, rebuke him. If he repents, forgive him. If he sins against you seven times in the day, and seven times returns, saying, 'I repent,' you shall forgive him."

The apostles said to the Lord, "Increase our faith."

The Lord said, "If you had faith like a grain of mustard seed, you would tell this sycamore tree, 'Be uprooted, and be planted in the sea,' and it would obey you. But who is there among you, having a servant ploughing or keeping sheep, that will say, when he comes in from the field, 'Come immediately and sit down at the table,' and will not rather tell him, 'Prepare my supper, clothe yourself properly, and serve me, while I eat and drink. Afterward you shall eat and drink'? Does he thank that servant because he did the things that were commanded? I think not. Even so you also, when you have done all the things that are commanded you, say, 'We are unworthy servants. We have done our duty.'"

∞∞○∞∞

Lord God, I know you have planted faith in my heart. I ask you that you will teach me more about faith and how to walk in it. Please guide me and help me walk by faith and not by what I see. Help me to grow in faith as I read and listen to your word. I pray you will lead me in paths of righteousness. Let me never be responsible for encouraging someone to sin. Give me grace to encourage people to follow you, O Lord. I am your servant. Please help me to be faithful, in Jesus name, Amen.

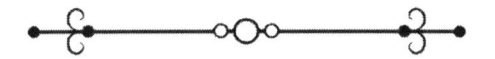

TEN HEALED OF LEPROSY

LUKE 17:11-19

As he was on his way to Jerusalem, he was passing along the borders of Samaria and Galilee. As he entered into a certain village, ten men who were lepers met him, who stood at a distance. They lifted up their voices, saying, "Jesus, Master, have mercy on us!"

When he saw them, he said to them, "Go and show yourselves to the priests." As they went, they were cleansed. One of them, when he saw that he was healed, turned back, glorifying God with a loud voice. He fell on his face at Jesus' feet, giving him thanks; and he was a Samaritan. Jesus answered, "Weren't the ten cleansed? But where are the nine? Were there none found who returned to give glory to God, except this stranger?" Then he said to him, "Get up, and go your way. Your faith has healed you."

Thank you Lord for your incredible grace and mercy in my life. Thank you for my home and family. Thank you for my church and the precious fellowship I have with those I meet with. Thank you for your daily provision. I never go without, as you provide my every need. I love you Lord. There is no-one like you. Only you knit the threads of our lives together into something beautiful, that brings you glory. Be lifted up O lord, my God. Let your glory shine forth and draw men to you. In the holy name of Jesus I ask. Amen.

The Coming of the Kingdom of God

Luke 17:20-37

Being asked by the Pharisees when God's Kingdom would come, he answered them, "God's Kingdom doesn't come with observation; neither will they say, 'Look, here!' or, 'Look, there!' for behold, God's Kingdom is within you."

He said to the disciples, "The days will come, when you will desire to see one of the days of the Son of Man, and you will not see it. They will tell you, 'Look, here!' or 'Look, there!' Don't go away, nor follow after them, for as the lightning, when it flashes out of the one part under the sky, shines to the other part under the sky; so will the Son of Man be in his day. But first, he must suffer many things and be rejected by this generation. As it was in the days of Noah, even so will it be also in the days of the Son of Man. They ate, they drank, they married, they were given in marriage, until the day that Noah entered into the ship, and the flood came, and destroyed them all. Likewise, even as it was in the days of Lot: they ate, they drank, they bought, they sold, they planted, they built; but in the day that Lot went out from Sodom, it rained fire and sulfur from the sky, and destroyed them all. It will be the same way in the day that the Son of Man is revealed. In that day, he who will be on the housetop, and his goods in the house, let him not go down to take them away. Let him who is in the field likewise not turn back. Remember Lot's wife! Whoever seeks to save his life loses it, but whoever loses his life preserves it. I tell you, in that night there will be two people in one bed. The one will be taken, and the other will be left. There will be two grinding grain together. One will be taken, and the other will be left."

They, answering, asked him, "Where, Lord?"

He said to them, "Where the body is, there will the vultures also be gathered together."

Father, your dwelling place is in heaven. The earth is your footstool, and yet your kingdom is among us. Your kingdom has come into my life and the lives of countless others. It grows every second as you prepare hearts to receive your grace. What words are there to express gratitude for such honour among us? *Thank you* seems so small a thing to say. But I do thank you. I know that I was lost, but now I am found. And Father, I long for the day when I will see you face to face. I long for the day when earthly pain and suffering cease. I long for Jesus to come back and we might dwell with you forever. Let your name be lifted up. Amen

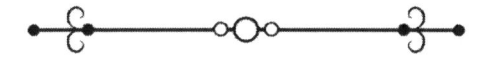

THE PARABLE OF THE PERSISTENT WIDOW

LUKE 18:1-8

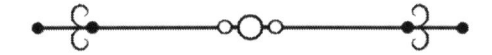

He also spoke a parable to them that they must always pray, and not give up, saying, "There was a judge in a certain city who didn't fear God, and didn't respect man. A widow was in that city, and she often came to him, saying, 'Defend me from my adversary!' He wouldn't for a while, but afterward he said to himself, 'Though I neither fear God, nor respect man, yet because this widow bothers me, I will defend her, or else she will wear me out by her continual coming.'"

The Lord said, "Listen to what the unrighteous judge says. Won't God avenge his chosen ones, who are crying out to him day and night, and yet he exercises patience with them? I tell you that he will avenge them quickly. Nevertheless, when the Son of Man comes, will he find faith on the earth?"

Lord Jesus, you taught your disciples to pray, and not to give up. As I read this passage I know you are speaking to me too. I know that I give up too easily. I don't 'follow through' in prayer. Please help me to be faithful in praying until I see your answer. Help me to be faithful in prayer for my children and family. Help me to be faithful in praying for your kingdom to come into the lives of my neighbours and friends. Please guide me and help to be consistent in spending time with you. In your holy name I pray, Amen.

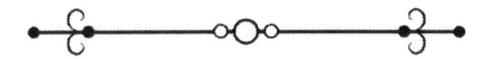

THE PARABLE OF THE PHARISEE AND THE TAX COLLECTOR

LUKE 18:9-17

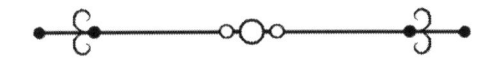

He spoke also this parable to certain people who were convinced of their own righteousness, and who despised all others. "Two men went up into the temple to pray; one was a Pharisee, and the other was a tax collector. The Pharisee stood and prayed to himself like this: 'God, I thank you, that I am not like the rest of men, extortionists, unrighteous, adulterers, or even like this tax collector. I fast twice a week. I give tithes of all that I get.' But the tax collector, standing far away, wouldn't even lift up his eyes to heaven, but beat his breast, saying, 'God, be merciful to me, a sinner!' I tell you, this man went down to his house justified rather than the other; for everyone who exalts himself will be humbled, but he who humbles himself will be exalted."

They were also bringing their babies to him, that he might touch them. But when the disciples saw it, they rebuked them. Jesus summoned them, saying, "Allow the little children to come to me, and don't hinder them, for God's Kingdom belongs to such as these. Most certainly, I tell you, whoever doesn't receive God's Kingdom like a little child, he will in no way enter into it."

○○○─○─○○○

Lord Jesus, I know that there is no-one righteous. We are all sinners. Not one of us is worthy to enter your presence, no matter how 'good' we may be. Yet in your great mercy you came, so that whoever believes in you will be righteous before the Father. What an incredible gift you have given us. We deserve death, yet you have given us life. We deserve to be punished, yet you took the punishment yourself. We were blind and deaf to your call, yet you opened our eyes and gave us ears to hear. You, O Lord, are wonderful, full of grace and majesty. Glory be to your holy name. Amen

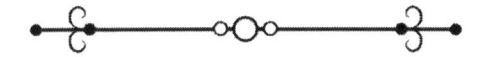

THE RICH RULER

LUKE 18:18-30

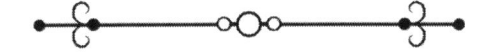

A certain ruler asked him, saying, "Good Teacher, what shall I do to inherit eternal life?"

Jesus asked him, "Why do you call me good? No one is good, except one—God. You know the commandments: 'Don't commit adultery,' 'Don't murder,' 'Don't steal,' 'Don't give false testimony,' 'Honour your father and your mother.' "

He said, "I have observed all these things from my youth up."

When Jesus heard these things, he said to him, "You still lack one thing. Sell all that you have, and distribute it to the poor. You will have treasure in heaven. Come, follow me."

But when he heard these things, he became very sad, for he was very rich.

Jesus, seeing that he became very sad, said, "How hard it is for those who have riches to enter into God's Kingdom! For it is easier for a camel to enter in through a needle's eye, than for a rich man to enter into God's Kingdom."

Those who heard it said, "Then who can be saved?"

But he said, "The things which are impossible with men are possible with God."

Peter said, "Look, we have left everything, and followed you."

He said to them, "Most certainly I tell you, there is no one who has left house, or wife, or brothers, or parents, or children, for God's Kingdom's sake, who will not receive many times more in this time, and in the world to come, eternal life."

ooo○ooo

Lord Jesus, you told the rich man and all those around him, how difficult it was to enter the kingdom of God. So much so that they asked you, "Who can be saved?" We know how short of your standards we fall. Yet you say, "What is impossible with man is possible with God." It is such a relief to know that you made a way, and that it doesn't depend on us. We don't have to strive to earn anything. You have done it all. I lift up your holy name, Lord Jesus. Only you are worthy to receive all glory, honour and praise. I was once lost, but you took me out of darkness and placed me in your kingdom of light. Only you can save. You are my Lord and King and I love you. Amen.

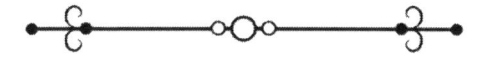

JESUS AGAIN PREDICTS HIS DEATH

LUKE 18:31-34

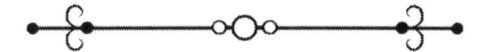

He took the twelve aside, and said to them, "Behold, we are going up to Jerusalem, and all the things that are written through the prophets concerning the Son of Man will be completed. For he will be delivered up to the Gentiles, will be mocked, treated shamefully, and spit on. They will scourge and kill him. On the third day, he will rise again."

They understood none of these things. This saying was hidden from them, and they didn't understand the things that were said.

O God, I love your word. I love how through the ages you reveal your plans to the prophets before things happen. No other book ever written does this. I love how you reveal yourself in so many different ways. Please help me understand as I read. I want to see every significant thing. Let there remain nothing hidden. I want to know you more. I want to understand more. Continue to reveal yourself, Lord God. You are my Saviour, Redeemer and my King. Amen

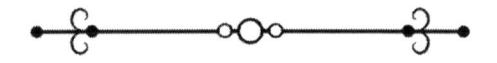

A Blind Beggar Receives His Sight

Luke 18:35-43

As he came near Jericho, a certain blind man sat by the road, begging. Hearing a multitude going by, he asked what this meant. They told him that Jesus of Nazareth was passing by. He cried out, "Jesus, you son of David, have mercy on me!" Those who led the way rebuked him, that he should be quiet; but he cried out all the more, "You son of David, have mercy on me!"

Standing still, Jesus commanded him to be brought to him. When he had come near, he asked him, "What do you want me to do?"

He said, "Lord, that I may see again."

Jesus said to him, "Receive your sight. Your faith has healed you."

Immediately he received his sight, and followed him, glorifying God. All the people, when they saw it, praised God.

Lord Jesus, when I read this passage, I see not just the blind man's great faith, but also his bold perseverance. He didn't care what people thought. He just wanted you to touch him. I would really like to be like this. I care too much what people think. I want to walk with you in boldness and faith. Please forgive me the times I have retreated from speaking about you because of fear what others might think. In reading of this blind man's faith I can see how thousands of years later his boldness has affected my life and the lives of countless others. I want my life to count too. You were glorified because of his perseverance. Please help me, so I might also be bold and persevere, and bring you glory. Amen.

ZACCHAEUS THE TAX COLLECTOR

LUKE 19:1-10

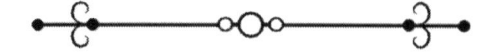

He entered and was passing through Jericho. There was a man named Zacchaeus. He was a chief tax collector, and he was rich. He was trying to see who Jesus was, and couldn't because of the crowd, because he was short.

He ran on ahead, and climbed up into a sycamore tree to see him, for he was going to pass that way.

When Jesus came to the place, he looked up and saw him, and said to him, "Zacchaeus, hurry and come down, for today I must stay at your house." He hurried, came down, and received him joyfully. When they saw it, they all murmured, saying, "He has gone in to lodge with a man who is a sinner."

Zacchaeus stood and said to the Lord, "Behold, Lord, half of my goods I give to the poor. If I have wrongfully exacted anything of anyone, I restore four times as much."

Jesus said to him, "Today, salvation has come to this house, because he also is a son of Abraham. For the Son of Man came to seek and to save that which was lost."

◦◦◦○◦◦◦

Lord Jesus, you are not one to look at outward appearances, but you look at the heart. You see past sin and see our deepest longings. Please give me discernment with my family and friends. Please help me to discern what is going on in their heart, and not to judge based on appearances. Give me wisdom to share your great love with those who need to hear. You came to save those who are lost. Lead me to them, O God, and I will tell them about you. Let your kingdom come in their lives for your name's sake, Amen.

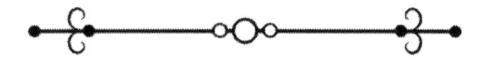

THE PARABLE OF THE TEN MINAS

LUKE 19:11-28

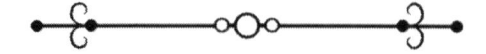

As they heard these things, he went on and told a parable, because he was near Jerusalem, and they supposed that God's Kingdom would be revealed immediately. He said therefore, "A certain nobleman went into a far country to receive for himself a kingdom, and to return. He called ten servants of his, and gave them ten mina coins, and told them, 'Conduct business until I come.' But his citizens hated him, and sent an envoy after him, saying, 'We don't want this man to reign over us.'

"When he had come back again, having received the kingdom, he commanded these servants, to whom he had given the money, to be called to him, that he might know what they had gained by conducting business. The first came before him, saying, 'Lord, your mina has made ten more minas.'

"He said to him, 'Well done, you good servant! Because you were found faithful with very little, you shall have authority over ten cities.'

"The second came, saying, 'Your mina, Lord, has made five minas.'

"So he said to him, 'And you are to be over five cities.' Another came, saying, 'Lord, behold, your mina, which I kept laid away in a handkerchief, for I feared you, because you are an exacting man. You take up that which you didn't lay down, and reap that which you didn't sow'

"He said to him, 'Out of your own mouth I will judge you, you wicked servant! You knew that I am an exacting man, taking up that which I didn't lay down, and reaping that which I didn't sow Then why didn't you deposit my money in the bank, and at my coming, I might have earned interest on it?' He said to those who stood by, 'Take the mina away from him, and give it to him who has the ten minas.'

"They said to him, 'Lord, he has ten minas!' 'For I tell you that to everyone who has, will more be given; but from him who doesn't have, even that which he has will be taken away from him. But bring those enemies of mine who didn't want me to reign over them here, and kill them before me.'" Having said these things, he went on ahead, going up to Jerusalem.

∞∞⃝∞∞

O God, the desire of my heart is to hear you say to me, "Well done, good and faithful servant." To live for you, to please you, to honour you, to love you is all I want to do. There is nothing else of any worth except these things. Thank you for your work in my life. Thank you for changing me. I know I can't change myself. Give me more hunger for righteousness. Soften my heart that I might hear you. Give me the desire to do your will. Let me be found faithful, when I stand before you, O God. In Jesus name I pray, Amen.

THE TRIUMPHAL ENTRY

LUKE 19:29-44

When he came near to Bethsphage and Bethany, at the mountain that is called Olivet, he sent two of his disciples, saying, "Go your way into the village on the other side, in which, as you enter, you will find a colt tied, which no man had ever sat upon. Untie it, and bring it. If anyone asks you, 'Why are you untying it?' say to him: 'The Lord needs it.'"

Those who were sent went away, and found things just as he had told them. As they were untying the colt, its owners said to them, "Why are you untying the colt?" They said, "The Lord needs it." They brought it to Jesus. They threw their cloaks on the colt, and set Jesus on them. As he went, they spread their cloaks on the road. As he was now getting near, at the descent of the Mount of Olives, the whole multitude of the disciples began to rejoice and praise God with a loud voice for all the mighty works which they had seen, saying, "Blessed is the King who comes in the name of the Lord! Peace in heaven, and glory in the highest!"

Some of the Pharisees from the multitude said to him, "Teacher, rebuke your disciples!"

He answered them, "I tell you that if these were silent, the stones would cry out."

When he came near, he saw the city and wept over it, saying, "If you, even you, had known today the things which belong to your peace! But now, they are hidden from your eyes. For the days will come on you, when your enemies will throw up a barricade against you, surround you, hem you in on every side, and will dash you and your children within you to the ground. They will not leave in you one stone on another, because you didn't know the time of your visitation."

<hr />

Lord, as I read this passage, I am struck by the instant obedience of the colt owner. He didn't argue, or question, or refuse. He heard you needed the colt, and he gave it to you. This is how I want to be. Please give me a willing heart to carry out those tasks you have given me to do. Forgive me for the times I have grown weary serving and just want a way out. Give me grace to serve. This is what I want, but I know that many times it is not what I do. Even if I do obey you, many times it is with a wrong attitude. Please forgive me. Help me remember whom I serve, in Jesus name, Amen.

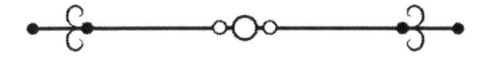

JESUS AT THE TEMPLE

LUKE 19:45-48

He entered into the temple, and began to drive out those who bought and sold in it, saying to them, "It is written, 'My house is a house of prayer,' but you have made it a 'den of robbers'!"

He was teaching daily in the temple, but the chief priests and the scribes and the leading men among the people sought to destroy him. They couldn't find what they might do, for all the people hung on to every word that he said.

Your word, O God, is the most precious gift we have ever been given. To have it written down so that we might read it over and over; to be able to study and ponder over it; to pray and to listen, and to know that you speak, is indescribable. It is beyond understanding why you care so much for us. Who is like you, O Lord, my God? There is none like you.

THE AUTHORITY OF JESUS QUESTIONED

LUKE 20:1-8

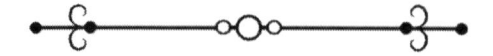

On one of those days, as he was teaching the people in the temple and preaching the Good News, the priests and scribes came to him with the elders. They asked him, "Tell us: by what authority do you do these things? Or who is giving you this authority?"

He answered them, "I also will ask you one question. Tell me: the baptism of John, was it from heaven, or from men?"

They reasoned with themselves, saying, "If we say, 'From heaven,' he will say, 'Why didn't you believe him?' But if we say, 'From men,' all the people will stone us, for they are persuaded that John was a prophet." They answered that they didn't know where it was from.

Jesus said to them, "Neither will I tell you by what authority I do these things."

Father, I pray for my friends and family who don't know you. Please open their eyes and understanding so they might see you. I pray that all doubt and fear and unbelief might leave them. Instead, I ask that they might be filled with faith. I ask that they might be convicted of their sin, and their need of a Saviour. O God, give me opportunity to speak to them. Help me find the right words to say, in Jesus name, Amen.

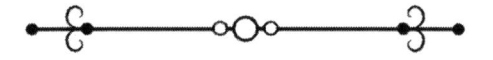

THE PARABLE OF THE TENANTS

LUKE 20:9-19

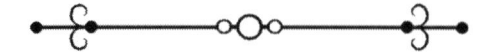

He began to tell the people this parable. "A man planted a vineyard, and rented it out to some farmers, and went into another country for a long time. At the proper season, he sent a servant to the farmers to collect his share of the fruit of the vineyard. But the farmers beat him, and sent him away empty. He sent yet another servant, and they also beat him, and treated him shamefully, and sent him away empty. He sent yet a third, and they also wounded him, and threw him out. The lord of the vineyard said, 'What shall I do? I will send my beloved son. It may be that seeing him, they will respect him.'

"But when the farmers saw him, they reasoned among themselves, saying, 'This is the heir. Come, let's kill him, that the inheritance may be ours.' They threw him out of the vineyard, and killed him. What therefore will the lord of the vineyard do to them? He will come and destroy these farmers, and will give the vineyard to others."

When they heard it, they said, "May it never be!"

But he looked at them, and said, "Then what is this that is written,

'The stone which the builders rejected,
the same was made the chief cornerstone?'
Everyone who falls on that stone will be broken to pieces,
but it will crush whomever it falls on to dust."

The chief priests and the scribes sought to lay hands on him that very hour, but they feared the people—for they knew he had spoken this parable against them.

∞∞○∞∞

Lord God, thank you for your patience and your goodness. Thank you that you have never given up your plan of redemption. No matter how we behave, you sent your Son. After we rejected all your prophets, your warnings and signs, you STILL sent your Son. Thank you for this great salvation. Thank you that you never gave up. Your work in me WILL be completed. Your work in the Church WILL be completed. Your plans and purposes always come to pass. Nothing can stand against them. Great is your name, O Lord. Great are your deeds, my God.

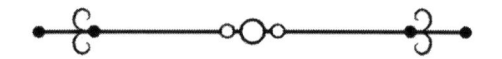

Paying Taxes to Caesar

Luke 20:20-26

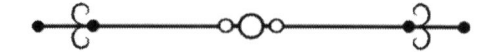

They watched him, and sent out spies, who pretended to be righteous, that they might trap him in something he said, so as to deliver him up to the power and authority of the governor. They asked him, "Teacher, we know that you say and teach what is right, and aren't partial to anyone, but truly teach the way of God. Is it lawful for us to pay taxes to Caesar, or not?"

But he perceived their craftiness, and said to them, "Why do you test me? Show me a denarius. Whose image and inscription are on it?"

They answered, "Caesar's."

He said to them, "Then give to Caesar the things that are Caesar's, and to God the things that are God's."

They weren't able to trap him in his words before the people. They marveled at his answer, and were silent.

Father, I ask you for wisdom and knowledge. Help me to understand your word when I read it. Bring books across my path that I might learn more about you. Not just to learn, but to remember. And not just to remember, but to be able to share my faith with others. Give me the words to say to those who doubt your existence. Help me to confound those questions designed to bring your name low. Let my words be full of grace and wisdom, and let them point to you. In Jesus name, Amen.

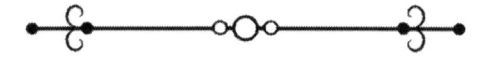

THE RESURRECTION AND MARRIAGE

LUKE 20:27-40

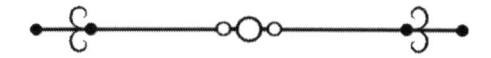

Some of the Sadducees came to him, those who deny that there is a resurrection. They asked him, "Teacher, Moses wrote to us that if a man's brother dies having a wife, and he is childless, his brother should take the wife, and raise up children for his brother. There were therefore seven brothers. The first took a wife, and died childless. The second took her as wife, and he died childless. The third took her, and likewise the seven all left no children, and died. Afterward the woman also died. Therefore in the resurrection whose wife of them will she be? For the seven had her as a wife."

Jesus said to them, "The children of this age marry, and are given in marriage. But those who are considered worthy to attain to that age and the resurrection from the dead, neither marry, nor are given in marriage. For they can't die any more, for they are like the angels, and are children of God, being children of the resurrection. But that the dead are raised, even Moses showed at the bush, when he called the Lord 'The God of Abraham, the God of Isaac, and the God of Jacob.' Now he is not the God of the dead, but of the living, for all are alive to him."

Some of the scribes answered, "Teacher, you speak well." They didn't dare to ask him any more questions.

Thank you Lord that I am one of those who will be in this resurrection. I can't imagine what it will be like to live a life where death is not present. It is beyond understanding to think of living in a place where there is no unhappiness or pain. I am your child, O God. You are my Father and I long for the day when I will see you face to face.

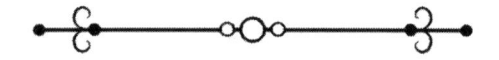

Whose Son Is the Christ?

Luke 20:41-47

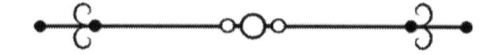

He said to them, "Why do they say that the Christ is David's son? David himself says in the book of Psalms,

'The Lord said to my Lord,

"Sit at my right hand,

until I make your enemies the footstool of your feet."'

"David therefore calls him Lord, so how is he his son?"

In the hearing of all the people, he said to his disciples, "Beware of those scribes who like to walk in long robes, and love greetings in the marketplaces, the best seats in the synagogues, and the best places at feasts; who devour widows' houses, and for a pretence make long prayers: these will receive greater condemnation."

Lord Jesus, by your Spirit you created the heavens and the earth. Your power sustains life and keeps the stars in place. Yet you humbled yourself and became a man, with all our weaknesses and vulnerability. O God, let your character be mirrored in me. I pray for a humble and contrite heart. Give me awareness when I am proud – that I might repent. I don't want a hint of pride in my life. I ask this in your holy name, Amen.

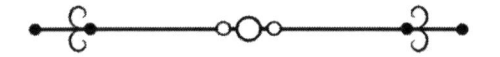

The Widow's Offering

Luke 21:1-4

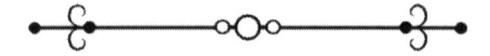

He looked up, and saw the rich people who were putting their gifts into the treasury. He saw a certain poor widow casting in two small brass coins. He said, "Truly I tell you, this poor widow put in more than all of them, for all these put in gifts for God from their abundance, but she, out of her poverty, put in all that she had to live on."

Lord, you said that you feed the birds of the air and clothe the grass of the field. They do not sow or reap or store in barns because you look after them. You told us not to worry about our lives for you are our provider. I pray that I will never be afraid of tithing or giving money to the needy. I am not my provider. You are. I pray for a generous and giving heart. Help me to trust your promise to provide for me, just as this widow did. In Jesus name, Amen.

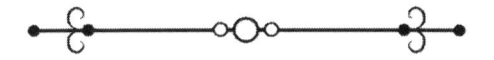

Signs of the End of the Age

Luke 21:5-38

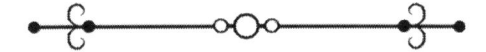

As some were talking about the temple and how it was decorated with beautiful stones and gifts, he said, "As for these things which you see, the days will come, in which there will not be left here one stone on another that will not be thrown down."

They asked him, "Teacher, so when will these things be? What is the sign that these things are about to happen?"

He said, "Watch out that you don't get led astray, for many will come in my name, saying, 'I am he,' and, 'The time is at hand.' Therefore don't follow them. When you hear of wars and disturbances, don't be terrified, for these things must happen first, but the end won't come immediately."

Then he said to them, "Nation will rise against nation, and kingdom against kingdom. There will be great earthquakes, famines, and plagues in various places. There will be terrors and great signs from heaven. But before all these things, they will lay their hands on you and will persecute you, delivering you up to synagogues and prisons, bringing you before kings and governors for my name's sake. It will turn out as a testimony for you. Settle it therefore in your hearts not to meditate beforehand how to answer, for I will give you a mouth and wisdom which all your adversaries will not be able to withstand or to contradict. You will be handed over even by parents, brothers, relatives, and friends. They will cause some of you to be put to death. You will be hated by all men for my name's sake. And not a hair of your head will perish.

"By your endurance you will win your lives.

"But when you see Jerusalem surrounded by armies, then know that its desolation is at hand. Then let those who are in Judea flee to the mountains. Let those who are in the middle of her depart. Let those who are in the country not enter therein. For these are days of vengeance, that all things which are written may be fulfilled. Woe to those who are pregnant and to those who nurse infants in those days! For there will be great distress in the land, and wrath to this people. They will fall by the edge of the sword, and will be led captive into all the nations. Jerusalem will be trampled down by the Gentiles, until the times of the Gentiles are fulfilled. There will be signs in the sun, moon, and stars; and on the earth *anxiety of nations, in perplexity for the roaring of the sea and the waves; men fainting for fear, and for expectation of the things which are coming on the world: for the powers of the heavens will be shaken. Then they will see the Son of Man coming in a cloud with power and great glory. But when these things begin to happen, look up, and lift up your heads, because your redemption is near."*

He told them a parable. "See the fig tree, and all the trees. When they are already budding, you see it and know by your own selves that the summer is already near. Even so you also, when you see these things happening, know that God's Kingdom is near. Most certainly I tell you, this generation will not pass away until all things are accomplished. Heaven and earth will pass away, but my words will by no means pass away.

"So be careful, or your hearts will be loaded down with carousing, drunkenness, and cares of this life, and that day will come on you suddenly. For it will come like a snare on all those who dwell on the surface of all the earth. Therefore be watchful all the time, praying that you may be counted worthy to escape all these things that will happen, and to stand before the Son of Man."

Every day Jesus was teaching in the temple, and every night he would go out and spend the night on the mountain that is called Olivet. All the people came early in the morning to him in the temple to hear him.

―◦◦◦―◯―◦◦◦―

Lord, as I read this passage, what stands out to me are the words, "By standing firm you will gain life." Please help me to stand firm on your word when it seems my life is falling apart. When trouble surrounds me, help me to remember you are my foundation. You are the only thing in my life that is unshakeable. Give me grace not to doubt. Fill my thoughts when it *seems* you are not near. Let your truth be foremost in my life, especially when I feel dry and weary. Thank you that you have promised to never leave me or forsake me. Thank you that you walk with me through the valley of the shadow of death. Thank you that you comfort and protect me. Amen.

JUDAS AGREES TO BETRAY JESUS

LUKE 22:1-6

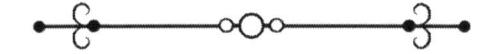

Now the feast of unleavened bread, which is called the Passover, was approaching. The chief priests and the scribes sought how they might put him to death, for they feared the people. Satan entered into Judas, who was also called Iscariot, who was counted with the twelve.

He went away, and talked with the chief priests and captains about how he might deliver him to them. They were glad, and agreed to give him money. He consented, and sought an opportunity to deliver him to them in the absence of the multitude.

Father, I am reminded that we are commanded to love you with all our heart, soul, mind and strength. Somewhere along the line, money became more important to Judas than loving you. Deliver me from temptation, O God. Give me grace to stand firm when things of the world seem to grow important. I ask that you will increase my desire for your word. Help me to feed on it daily so I might be filled with the knowledge of you. I ask forgiveness for the times I have made other things more important than you. I love you Lord and want my life to reflect your glory. I ask this in Jesus name, Amen.

PASSOVER PREPARATIONS

LUKE 22:7-13

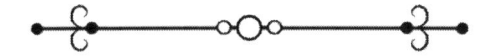

The day of unleavened bread came, on which the Passover must be sacrificed. Jesus sent Peter and John, saying, "Go and prepare the Passover for us, that we may eat."

They said to him, "Where do you want us to prepare?"

He said to them, "Behold, when you have entered into the city, a man carrying a pitcher of water will meet you. Follow him into the house which he enters. Tell the master of the house, 'The Teacher says to you, "Where is the guest room, where I may eat the Passover with my disciples?"' He will show you a large, furnished upper room. Make preparations there."

They went, found things as Jesus had told them, and they prepared the Passover.

O God, I pray for an obedient heart like these disciples and like the man to whom the house belonged. I pray for obedience without question. I want your will to be done in my life. You set good works before me to do. I pray I will do them without hesitation and with a joyful heart. I pray I will serve my family with gladness. Let me not grow weary in serving my friends. Make me sensitive to their needs so that I might bless them. O God, I ask for *ears that hear* your Spirit, when I talk to my neighbours – so I might speak your word, that they might learn of your goodness. Be glorified in my life, O God. Amen.

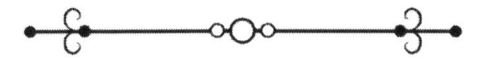

THE LAST SUPPER

LUKE 22:14-23

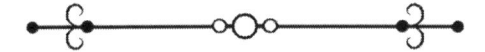

When the hour had come, he sat down with the twelve apostles. He said to them, "I have earnestly desired to eat this Passover with you before I suffer, for I tell you, I will no longer by any means eat of it until it is fulfilled in God's Kingdom." He received a cup, and when he had given thanks, he said, "Take this, and share it among yourselves, for I tell you, I will not drink at all again from the fruit of the vine, until God's Kingdom comes."

He took bread, and when he had given thanks, he broke, and gave it to them, saying, "This is my body which is given for you. Do this in memory of me." Likewise, he took the cup after supper, saying, "This cup is the new covenant in my blood, which is poured out for you. But behold, the hand of him who betrays me is with me on the table. The Son of Man indeed goes, as it has been determined, but woe to that man through whom he is betrayed!"

They began to question among themselves, which of them it was who would do this thing.

Thank you Lord that you have given us these symbols so we might constantly remember your work on the cross. Thank you for taking the punishment I deserve, so I might live eternity with you. You have taken my life and given me hope. Not just hope in this life, but you have a home prepared for me when this life is finished. I am so grateful. Amen

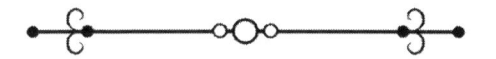

WHO IS THE GREATEST?

LUKE 22:24-30

There arose also a contention among them, which of them was considered to be greatest. He said to them, "The kings of the nations lord it over them, and those who have authority over them are called 'benefactors.' But not so with you. But one who is the greater among you, let him become as the younger, and one who is governing, as one who serves. For who is greater, one who sits at the table, or one who serves? Isn't it he who sits at the table? But I am among you as one who serves. But you are those who have continued with me in my trials. I confer on you a kingdom, even as my Father conferred on me, that you may eat and drink at my table in my Kingdom. You will sit on thrones, judging the twelve tribes of Israel."

Lord Jesus, I pray that you will root out every area of pride in my life. Forgive me for the times I have thought myself better than others. I pray that I might think constantly of your servant heart and your example to us. I want that humility of heart. I don't just want to serve with my actions only. I want to serve with humility of heart, truly loving those I am serving, even as you did. Cleanse my heart O God, and renew a right Spirit within me. In your holy name I pray, Amen.

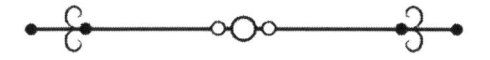

Jesus Predicts Peter's Denial

Luke 22:31-38

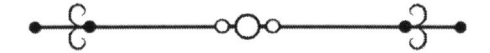

The Lord said, "Simon, Simon, behold, Satan asked to have all of you, that he might sift you as wheat, but I prayed for you, that your faith wouldn't fail. You, when once you have turned again, establish your brothers."

He said to him, "Lord, I am ready to go with you both to prison and to death!"

He said, "I tell you, Peter, the rooster will by no means crow today until you deny that you know me three times."

He said to them, "When I sent you out without purse, and wallet, and shoes, did you lack anything?"

They said, "Nothing."

Then he said to them, "But now, whoever has a purse, let him take it, and likewise a wallet. Whoever has none, let him sell his cloak, and buy a sword. For I tell you that this which is written must still be fulfilled in me: 'He was counted with transgressors.' For that which concerns me has an end."

They said, "Lord, behold, here are two swords."

He said to them, "That is enough."

∞∞◦○◦∞∞

Father, I know in this life we face many trials. I know you use them to teach us to persevere. When I go through hard times, I just want to run away and find the quickest and easiest way out. At the time of trial I never think you might be using it to work a change in me. Please help me to be more aware of your work in me, and not to fear times of trial. You promised never to leave or forsake us. I pray you will give me a faithful heart, no matter what events occur in my life. I want to learn to persevere and become mature in my faith. Teach me more about you, O God. I ask in Jesus name, Amen.

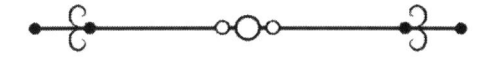

JESUS PRAYS ON THE MOUNT OF OLIVES

LUKE 22:39-53

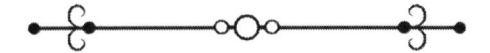

He came out, and went, as his custom was, to the Mount of Olives. His disciples also followed him. When he was at the place, he said to them, "Pray that you don't enter into temptation."

He was withdrawn from them about a stone's throw, and he knelt down and prayed, saying, "Father, if you are willing, remove this cup from me. Nevertheless, not my will, but yours, be done."

An angel from heaven appeared to him, strengthening him. Being in agony he prayed more earnestly. His sweat became like great drops of blood falling down on the ground.

When he rose up from his prayer, he came to the disciples, and found them sleeping because of grief, and said to them, "Why do you sleep? Rise and pray that you may not enter into temptation."

While he was still speaking, behold, a multitude, and he who was called Judas, one of the twelve, was leading them. He came near to Jesus to kiss him. But Jesus said to him, "Judas, do you betray the Son of Man with a kiss?"

When those who were around him saw what was about to happen, they said to him, "Lord, shall we strike with the sword?" A certain one of them struck the servant of the high priest, and cut off his right ear.

But Jesus answered, "Let me at least do this"—and he touched his ear, and healed him. Jesus said to the chief priests, captains of the temple, and elders, who had come against him, "Have you come out as against a robber, with swords and clubs? When I was with you in the temple daily, you didn't stretch out your hands against me. But this is your hour, and the power of darkness."

ooooOooo

Lord Jesus, you endured such anguish for our sake. There is nothing in my experience that can come close to helping me understand how you must have felt. You *chose* to do the Father's will. You created the universe, yet you allowed mortal man to bind you. You chose to allow him to lead you away – when with one word you could have made it all stop. You chose to be our sacrifice. What is there for me to do but to live my life honouring you. There is nothing for me to contribute to what you have done. Nothing except bow the knee and worship. Amen

PETER DISOWNS JESUS

LUKE 22:54-62

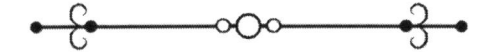

They seized him, and led him away, and brought him into the high priest's house. But Peter followed from a distance. When they had kindled a fire in the middle of the courtyard, and had sat down together, Peter sat among them. A certain servant girl saw him as he sat in the light, and looking intently at him, said, "This man also was with him."

He denied Jesus, saying, "Woman, I don't know him."

After a little while someone else saw him, and said, "You also are one of them!"

But Peter answered, "Man, I am not!"

After about one hour passed, another confidently affirmed, saying, "Truly this man also was with him, for he is a Galilean!"

But Peter said, "Man, I don't know what you are talking about!" Immediately, while he was still speaking, a rooster crowed. The Lord turned, and looked at Peter. Then Peter remembered the Lord's word, how he said to him, "Before the rooster crows you will deny me three times." He went out, and wept bitterly.

∞∞◯∞∞

Lord Jesus, as I read this passage I am so convicted of sin. Peter denied you surrounded by violence and the threat of death. Yet I have feared to tell people about you so as not to bring disapproval or ridicule on myself. I am so ashamed. Please forgive me. Please give me courage to speak boldly about what you have done. Fill me with your Spirit like the disciples on the day of Pentecost. I want to proclaim your gospel without fear. I want to see people's lives changed, and your name glorified. In Jesus name I pray, Amen.

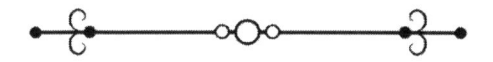

JESUS BEFORE THE ASSEMBLY OF ELDERS

LUKE 22:63-71

The men who held Jesus mocked him and beat him. Having blindfolded him, they struck him on the face and asked him, "Prophesy! Who is the one who struck you?" They spoke many other things against him, insulting him.

As soon as it was day, the assembly of the elders of the people were gathered together, both chief priests and scribes, and they led him away into their council, saying, "If you are the Christ, tell us."

But he said to them, "If I tell you, you won't believe, and if I ask, you will in no way answer me or let me go. From now on, the Son of Man will be seated at the right hand of the power of God."

They all said, "Are you then the Son of God?"

He said to them, "You say it, because I am."

They said, "Why do we need any more witness? For we ourselves have heard from his own mouth!"

Lord, I once stood before you as guilty as these men. I was as guilty as if I had mocked and blasphemed and beaten you myself. You spoke the truth, and yet each one of us raised a fist and proclaimed you a liar, as surely as if we had been there ourselves. We lived in darkness and loved it. Lord Jesus, you are the light of the world. You broke into our world of darkness and plucked us out of our filthy, hopeless, sinful lives and gave us hope. You changed my black blaspheming heart and made me righteous and holy. I can stand before God the Father without fear of His wrath, all because of you. My life is yours, O God. Do with it as you will. Let your name be lifted up and glorified forever. Amen.

JESUS BEFORE PILATE AND HEROD

LUKE 23:1-25

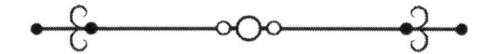

The whole company of them rose up and brought him before Pilate. They began to accuse him, saying, "We found this man perverting the nation, forbidding paying taxes to Caesar, and saying that he himself is Christ, a king."

Pilate asked him, "Are you the King of the Jews?"

He answered him, "So you say."

Pilate said to the chief priests and the multitudes, "I find no basis for a charge against this man."

But they insisted, saying, "He stirs up the people, teaching throughout all Judea, beginning from Galilee even to this place." But when Pilate heard Galilee mentioned, he asked if the man was a Galilean. When he found out that he was in Herod's jurisdiction, he sent him to Herod, who was also in Jerusalem during those days.

Now when Herod saw Jesus, he was exceedingly glad, for he had wanted to see him for a long time, because he had heard many things about him. He hoped to see some miracle done by him. He questioned him with many words, but he gave no answers. The chief priests and the scribes stood, vehemently accusing him. Herod with his soldiers humiliated him and mocked him. Dressing him in luxurious clothing, they sent him back to Pilate. Herod and Pilate became friends with each other that very day, for before that they were enemies with each other.

Pilate called together the chief priests, the rulers, and the people, and said to them, "You brought this man to me as one that perverts the people, and behold, having examined him before you, I found no basis for a charge against this man concerning those things of which you accuse him. Neither has Herod, for I sent you to him, and see, nothing worthy of death has been done by him. I will therefore chastise him and release him."

Now he had to release one prisoner to them at the feast. But they all cried out together, saying, "Away with this man! Release to us Barabbas!"— one who was thrown into prison for a certain revolt in the city, and for murder.

Then Pilate spoke to them again, wanting to release Jesus, but they shouted, saying, "Crucify! Crucify him!"

He said to them the third time, "Why? What evil has this man done? I have found no capital crime in him. I will therefore chastise him and release him." But they were urgent with loud voices, asking that he might be crucified. Their voices and the voices of the chief priests prevailed. Pilate decreed that what they asked for should be done. He released him who had been thrown into prison for insurrection and murder, for whom they asked, but he delivered Jesus up to their will.

ooo○ooo

Lord God, left to ourselves we are like that rebellious crowd. Until you changed us, we were against you. Our wish was only to please ourselves and not a thought given as to whether or not your will was being done. Lord Jesus, you are full of grace and mercy. We deserved your judgement, yet you withheld our punishment, and instead took it upon yourself. This is the gospel you have given us. As I think about this, all I can do is worship and adore you, O Lord my God.

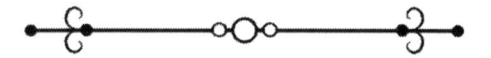

The Crucifixion

Luke 23:26-43

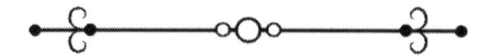

When they led him away, they grabbed one Simon of Cyrene, coming from the country, and laid on him the cross, to carry it after Jesus. A great multitude of the people followed him, including women who also mourned and lamented him. But Jesus, turning to them, said, "Daughters of Jerusalem, don't weep for me, but weep for yourselves and for your children. For behold, the days are coming in which they will say, 'Blessed are the barren, the wombs that never bore, and the breasts that never nursed.' Then they will begin to tell the mountains, 'Fall on us!' and tell the hills, 'Cover us.' For if they do these things in the green tree, what will be done in the dry?"

There were also others, two criminals, led with him to be put to death. When they came to the place that is called The Skull, they crucified him there with the criminals, one on the right and the other on the left.

Jesus said, "Father, forgive them, for they don't know what they are doing."

Dividing his garments among them, they cast lots. The people stood watching. The rulers with them also scoffed at him, saying, "He saved others. Let him save himself, if this is the Christ of God, his chosen one!"

The soldiers also mocked him, coming to him and offering him vinegar, and saying, "If you are the King of the Jews, save yourself!"

An inscription was also written over him in letters of Greek, Latin, and Hebrew: "THIS IS THE KING OF THE JEWS."

One of the criminals who was hanged insulted him, saying, "If you are the Christ, save yourself and us!"

But the other answered, and rebuking him said, "Don't you even fear God, seeing you are under the same condemnation? And we indeed justly, for we receive the due reward for our deeds, but this man has done nothing wrong." He said to Jesus, "Lord, remember me when you come into your Kingdom."

Jesus said to him, "Assuredly I tell you, today you will be with me in Paradise."

∞∞○∞∞

"Father, forgive them, for they know not what they do." O God, as I read this passage, I see your heart toward us. At this terrible time, you turned away from your Son and heaped our punishment on Him. The whole purpose of your wrath being poured out on

Jesus, and Him willingly submitting to it, was to bring about our forgiveness. How can I possibly put into words my gratitude for your loving compassion? My life belongs to you. Do with it as you will, to praise, to glorify and to honour you. Amen.

Jesus' Death and Burial

Luke 23:44-56

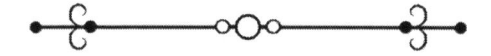

It was now about the sixth hour, and darkness came over the whole land until the ninth hour. The sun was darkened, and the veil of the temple was torn in two. Jesus, crying with a loud voice, said, "Father, into your hands I commit my spirit!" Having said this, he breathed his last.

When the centurion saw what was done, he glorified God, saying, "Certainly this was a righteous man." All the multitudes that came together to see this, when they saw the things that were done, returned home beating their breasts. All his acquaintances, and the women who followed with him from Galilee, stood at a distance, watching these things.

Behold, a man named Joseph, who was a member of the council, a good and righteous man (he had not consented to their counsel and deed), from Arimathaea, a city of the Jews, who was also waiting for God's Kingdom: this man went to Pilate, and asked for Jesus' body. He took it down, and wrapped it in a linen cloth, and laid him in a tomb that was cut in stone, where no one had ever been laid. It was the day of the Preparation, and the Sabbath was drawing near. The women, who had come with him out of Galilee, followed after, and saw the tomb, and how his body was laid. They returned, and prepared spices and ointments. On the Sabbath they rested according to the commandment.

∘∘∘◦○◦∘∘∘

...the veil of the temple was torn in two. What glorious words those are. Your purpose was fulfilled. Man could now enter the presence of God without sacrificing bulls and sheep. We could enter your presence freely without fear. Thank you. Thank you for saving me. Thank you for changing my life. Thank you for the promise of an eternity spent with you. Thank you.

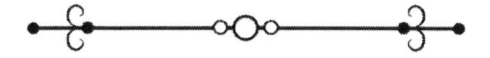

The Resurrection

Luke 24:1-12

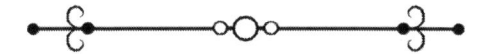

But on the first day of the week, at early dawn, they and some others came to the tomb, bringing the spices which they had prepared. They found the stone rolled away from the tomb. They entered in, and didn't find the Lord Jesus' body. While they were greatly perplexed about this, behold, two men stood by them in dazzling clothing. Becoming terrified, they bowed their faces down to the earth.

They said to them, "Why do you seek the living among the dead? He isn't here, but is risen. Remember what he told you when he was still in Galilee, saying that the Son of Man must be delivered up into the hands of sinful men, and be crucified, and the third day rise again?"

They remembered his words, returned from the tomb, and told all these things to the eleven, and to all the rest. Now they were Mary Magdalene, Joanna, and Mary the mother of James. The other women with them told these things to the apostles. These words seemed to them to be nonsense, and they didn't believe them. But Peter got up and ran to the tomb. Stooping and looking in, he saw the strips of linen lying by themselves, and he departed to his home, wondering what had happened.

ooo◯ooo

The women were *greatly perplexed* by not finding the body of Jesus in the tomb. Father, as I read this I am reminded that many times unexpected things happen. Things I thought should surely happen one way, either didn't happen, or something entirely different happened. I pray in those times, I will remember to trust in you. I ask that worry and fear won't be my first reaction, but rather a confidence that you are in control of my life. You are my foundation, but I so often forget. Help me to remember and trust. Forgive me my unbelief and cause my faith to grow, in Jesus name I ask, Amen.

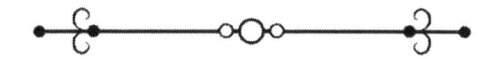

ON THE ROAD TO EMMAUS

LUKE 24:13-35

Behold, two of them were going that very day to a village named Emmaus, which was sixty stadia from Jerusalem. They talked with each other about all of these things which had happened. While they talked and questioned together, Jesus himself came near, and went with them. But their eyes were kept from recognizing him. He said to them, "What are you talking about as you walk, and are sad?"

One of them, named Cleopas, answered him, "Are you the only stranger in Jerusalem who doesn't know the things which have happened there in these days?"

He said to them, "What things?"

They said to him, "The things concerning Jesus, the Nazarene, who was a prophet mighty in deed and word before God and all the people; and how the chief priests and our rulers delivered him up to be condemned to death, and crucified him. But we were hoping that it was he who would redeem Israel. Yes, and besides all this, it is now the third day since these things happened. Also, certain women of our company amazed us, having arrived early at the tomb; and when they didn't find his body, they came saying that they had also seen a vision of angels, who said that he was alive. Some of us went to the tomb, and found it just like the women had said, but they didn't see him."

He said to them, "Foolish men, and slow of heart to believe in all that the prophets have spoken! Didn't the Christ have to suffer these things and to enter into his glory?" Beginning from Moses and from all the prophets, he explained to them in all the Scriptures the things concerning himself. They came near to the village, where they were going, and he acted like he would go further.

They urged him, saying, "Stay with us, for it is almost evening, and the day is almost over."

He went in to stay with them. When he had sat down at the table with them, he took the bread and gave thanks. Breaking it, he gave it to them. Their eyes were opened, and they recognized him, and he vanished out of their sight. They said to one another, "Weren't our hearts burning within us, while he spoke to us along the way, and while he opened the Scriptures to us?" They rose up that very hour, returned to Jerusalem, and found the eleven gathered together, and those who were with them, saying, "The

Lord is risen indeed, and has appeared to Simon!" They related the things that happened along the way, and how he was recognized by them in the breaking of the bread.

Lord God, I pray when things in life are bleak and hopeless, I will recognise that you are still working out your plans and purposes. No matter how things look, there is not a moment that you leave us on our own. As I walk with you, O God, build my faith. I ask that I might see beyond present circumstances to see you at work. Not just any work, but you work for the good of those who love you – and that includes me – at *all* times. I *will* trust in you and not lean on my own understanding. Amen

JESUS APPEARS TO THE DISCIPLES

LUKE 24:36-49

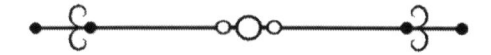

As they said these things, Jesus himself stood among them, and said to them, "Peace be to you."

But they were terrified and filled with fear, and supposed that they had seen a spirit.

He said to them, "Why are you troubled? Why do doubts arise in your hearts? See my hands and my feet, that it is truly me. Touch me and see, for a spirit doesn't have flesh and bones, as you see that I have." When he had said this, he showed them his hands and his feet. While they still didn't believe for joy, and wondered, he said to them, "Do you have anything here to eat?"

They gave him a piece of a broiled fish and some honeycomb. He took them, and ate in front of them. He said to them, "This is what I told you, while I was still with you, that all things which are written in the law of Moses, the prophets, and the psalms, concerning me must be fulfilled."

Then he opened their minds, that they might understand the Scriptures. He said to them, "Thus it is written, and thus it was necessary for the Christ to suffer and to rise from the dead the third day, and that repentance and remission of sins should be preached in his name to all the nations, beginning at Jerusalem. You are witnesses of these things. Behold, I send out the promise of my Father on you. But wait in the city of Jerusalem until you are clothed with power from on high."

―――○―――

Lord Jesus, the first words you said to the disciples after you had risen was, "*Peace to you.*" You have made peace between man and God. You have bestowed your peace upon us. I know that the minute I take my eyes of you and look at my circumstances, my peace disappears. Thank you for your work of reconciliation on the cross. Thank you for giving us this gift of peace. You also opened the disciples understanding so they might understand scripture. I ask you to do the same for me. I want a deep understanding of your word. I want to see your heart toward mankind in what is written. The desire of my heart is to know you more. I ask this in your holy name, Amen.

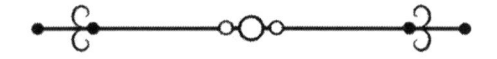

The Ascension

Luke 24:50-53

He led them out as far as Bethany, and he lifted up his hands, and blessed them. While he blessed them, he withdrew from them, and was carried up into heaven. They worshiped him, and returned to Jerusalem with great joy, and were continually in the temple, praising and blessing God. Amen.

You are my risen Saviour. You conquered death and gave us life. You bless and fill us with joy in your presence. My soul magnifies the Lord, and my spirit rejoices in God my Saviour. For you are mighty and have done great things for me. Holy is your name. You give salvation to your people. You forgive their sins and remove them as far as the East is from the West. Your tender mercy gives light to those who sit in darkness and guides our feet in the way of peace. Be glorified, O Lord my God. Amen.

ALSO BY BERENICE AGUILERA

Desiring God: 31 Prayers Seeking the Heart of God

"This book of scripture and prayers where amazing. It took the words I could never find and described the prayers from my heart. I was very grateful for this 31 day prayer journey. I would say if you love The Lord and need the words to pray and express your heart this is a book for you." (A L Tolzmann)

❖❖❖

"This was the best book on prayer that I've read. Each prayer seems like your own prayer. You could read and literally pray the prayer for yourself. I loved the simplicity of the prayers. They were heartfelt and stirring. The scriptures before each prayer was so appropriate; what an awesome way to lead into prayer. I recommend this book to anyone who wants to develop a meaningful prayer life." (Wilhelmina Farmer)

❖❖❖

"The Lord is awesome, greatly to be praised. This book confidently declares His handiwork. So uplifting. The selections remind us that there is no other like God." (Kindle Customer "Treasures for All")

❖❖❖

"This is a book I'll go back to often. I have always struggled with expressing myself to God through prayer. This book has helped me so much in learning how to pray to God the way I would like to. "(CB)

❖❖❖

"These prayers are from the bible...they have given me strength to speak to God in my own words. Those words used to come hard to me now after reciting these prayers I feel comfortable using my own words to honor God." (Midge)

Books edited by Berenice Aguilera

C H Spurgeon's Prayers (Illustrated) (Kindle version)

Books compiled by Berenice Aguilera

PRAYING THROUGH THE PROPHETS SERIES

Jeremiah & Lamentations
Ezekiel
Daniel
Hosea
Joel, Amos & Obadiah
Jonah, Micah, Nahum
Habakkuk, Zephaniah, Haggai
Zechariah & Malachi

Printed in Poland
by Amazon Fulfillment
Poland Sp. z o.o., Wrocław